SPIRITUAL SECRETS ABOUT SUICIDE

Bridge for Peace

SPIRITUAL SECRETS ABOUT SUICIDE

Annette M. Eckart

Bridge for Peace Publishers
Wading River, New York

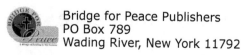 Bridge for Peace Publishers
PO Box 789
Wading River, New York 11792

Spiritual Secrets About Suicide
First Printing, October 2017
Copyright © 2017 by Annette M. Eckart
ISBN 978-0-9845306-5-6

Available through Bridge for Peace
PO Box 789, Wading River, NY 11792
Phone (631) 730-3982 fax (631) 730-3995
www.bridgeforpeace.org

Scriptures in this book include direct quotations, as
well as the author's adaptations, from various translations of the Holy Bible.

Cover Design by Kevin McKernan
Cover Photograph by Emily Scarbrough

Printed in the U. S. A.

Dedicated to
Jesus Christ
the only One
Who saves

Table of Contents

Tragedy

Pastor Frank stepped around the casket of the eighteen-year-old boy. John had died from a self-inflicted gunshot wound. High school students, neighbors, and family members—both local and from overseas—packed the funeral service to grieve and to comfort his parents and sister. Like medics at a disaster site working together to stop the bleeding. We held John's family tightly, but carefully, in the grip of our communal love.

Boys in the front pews wore football uniforms to honor John, their 6'2" captain whose broad shoulders, black hair, and robust appetite earned him the nickname "Big Bear." At the beginning of the season the community newspaper quoted coach Shay as saying John's attitude was "exemplary." I heard students' stories of how he intentionally befriended unpopular kids, made himself available to the lonely and the insecure. He was the designated driver, whether kids needed a ride for football practice or a party. His father Dennis said, "I used to give him a hard time about all the gas he used and he would say, 'Dad, these guys need a ride, it's so important.'"

My husband Ed and I knew John's aunt and uncle and saw him occasionally at their family parties or at church where he helped out at Sunday school every few weeks. We noted his polite self-assurance, unusual for a boy his age. We heard he recently visited the State University of New York at Cortland with his Dad and arranged for fall semester entry.

Last Sunday, warm March sunshine hinted at a beautiful spring. John attended church solo and returned home to nosh on his favorite bagels, smoked salmon, and onions in the kitchen with his parents. Since his car was in the repair shop, he asked for his Dad's Jeep keys and texted friends to meet him at the local beach. He took the quick drive to the shore. Big Bear ended his life. And then his friends arrived. Whispers spread the shocking news through our community. Neighbors shook their heads in disbelief. *Not again.*

Three months earlier a fourteen-year-old freshman boy, a well-liked varsity wrestler, left his home for a 10 a.m. run and didn't return. Search parties of neighbors and friends scoured the area until the next morning at 8 a.m. when police found his body in the woods. Suicide. Two weeks later another local student, a fifteen year old girl, died by suicide.

John's wake took place at the community funeral parlor. Ed and I arrived early, but a line had already formed outside the building. It continued throughout the hours of visitation. The empty space John left was filled with unanswerable questions, numbing shock, and inconsolable grieving.

I heard his mother say, "He slept a bit more than usual last week." But popular, athletic teenagers periodically need extra sleep. Family and friends asked themselves the tormenting question: *Did I miss something?* But John never showed the typical signs that raise concerns about suicide. I listened to men and women repeat the same phrases. "Doesn't make sense." "Incomprehensible." "The pastor is really shook up. Said he never saw it coming." "The son every father would want to have."

I kept silent as they expressed their confusion. I felt the sense of a tragic, irreplaceable loss, but didn't identify with their total bewilderment. Perhaps it was because I had a different experience of the power of suicidal suggestions.

People crowded into the church for John's 10 a.m. funeral. Those with and without religious convictions came. Some held tightly to their faith, others never thought about God. Whether they were Christian believers, disinterested in church, or even opposed to religion, people attended. An uncommon silence in the church became progressively oppressive. It was as though the emotionally exhausted congregation had unanimously consented to stifle all expressions of grief. High school girls sat stiff in their seats. A boy in a blue and white football jacket, elbows on his knees, face in his hands, wiped his silent tears.

John's father, Dennis, waited in the back of the church. A former New York City fire fighter, he had lost many of his colleagues in the Twin Towers collapse. He helped restore safety after 9/11 and one year later he retired.

The soloist opened her hymnal and the congregation stood. Dennis, assisted by family members, wheeled his son's dark wood coffin down the aisle.

In the middle of his sermon the pastor surprised us. He pointed midway back on the left side of the church. He said, "Have you noticed the empty seat there?" Like those near me, I turned around to look at the pew on the other side of the aisle. A single empty space at the end of the row was unoccupied in the full church. "That was John's usual seat in his usual pew," the pastor continued.

People in attendance from many different towns neither knew about John's usual place in church, nor did we intentionally leave his customary seat empty. Two girls looked at each other and raised their eyebrows as if to say, "This is strange." Others hunched their shoulders as if touched by an eerie chill. Some sensed it was a matter of supernatural design, affirming John was still with us. Not in the form we recognized, but among us nonetheless.

The bishop saved his remarks for the close of the funeral service. He stepped forward and looked at us, visibly gathering strength for the task ahead.

"Do not define John's life by *this* one moment," the bishop urged. "John is now in the heart of God. He now sees life through the heart of God. John now sees you from that perspective. I want you to think about this. As he looks at you today, what would he say to you?"

Fresh tears filled my eyes. I knew what God's heart was for me this morning. It was time to disclose what I had been taught. Time to reveal the spiritual secrets about suicide and stop the lies.

———◆———

When the pastor pointed out the empty seat left of the center aisle as John's usual seat, I heard a stir in the congregation. From the expressions on different faces, I could imagine reactions and questions. *Okay, so there is an empty place. Coincidence. What about it? Why is the pastor pointing it out? What is he suggesting?*

I was comfortable, even comforted, with the thought of John sitting among us. I know there is a spiritual realm where those who have died continue to live. And they are not the only ones alive in the vast spiritual realm. The deliberate opening of my own spirit to an unseen dimension resulted in divine encounters that eventually revealed secret spiritual realities about suicide.

Lies that dismiss the reality of powerful spiritual influences create a dangerous void. Many, tricked by deceptions, have tripped and fallen into dark emotional pits. Many uninstructed in spiritual truth lose hope of escape from despair. I recall a conversation I had with a professional in school administration.

She said, "We all received an early morning telephone call advising us to come in and meet in the high school cafeteria. Something had to be very wrong, but we didn't know what had happened. Everyone was anxious. The administrator announced that another student had committed suicide. It was terrible. This student had been treated medically and was on suicide watch, but it wasn't enough. No one knows what to do. I *know* this is a spiritual problem, but in school we can't talk about it," she said frustrated.

> Tricked by deceptions, many have tripped and fallen into dark emotional pits.

"And we have other students on suicide watch. Plus, we have students with anxiety and panic disorders. Some have home tutors since they cannot attend school. At times, students can be so paralyzed with fear that they cannot leave their room at home."

We agreed that one crucial component absent from the suicide prevention toolbox was knowledge of the spiritual world. Doctors, counsellors, hospital facilities, medications, and early warning symptom awareness are all vital. Health care providers agree that fostering relationships where feelings can be discussed is essential. Still, if we lack spiritual knowledge we are vulnerable. This became obvious to me as I interviewed Americans and Australians who have struggled with suicide.

> ...one crucial component absent from the suicide prevention toolbox was knowledge of the spiritual world.

Kristin said, "My husband was diagnosed with cancer. He wanted medical marijuana as a treatment. We moved out of state because it was illegal where we lived and I was afraid we would lose everything. He got into a lot of dark stuff. Our marriage got bad. I would drive around with my kids who were two and three years old and I'd hear a voice saying, 'Drive off the cliff with the kids. End it.'"

Kristin said suicide appeared reasonable, because of her circumstances. Knowledge of the spiritual realm educates us as to why these destructive suggestions appear good. We will explore that topic in a subsequent chapter. Kristin and other interviewees discovered power to overcome suggestions of self-destruction through spiritual awareness.

The spiritually awake understand war rages in the hidden world where opposing forces battle for human souls. We are born with a plan for a glorious life but wicked forces plot our destruction through any means, including suicide. *Spiritual Secrets About Suicide* can help you to understand hidden truth. May you read by the bright light of inner awareness.

———◆———

The Light of irrepressible brilliance pierces shrouds of darkness. The Light penetrates through walls of isolation. Tormented souls declare themselves dead inside, but the Light illuminates their inner tombs. The Light has a name—Jesus Christ. He enters in to be with us where we are and shadows dissolve.

For some of us, though our physical eyes have opened and we have climbed out from our beds, spiritually we are in a dead sleep. Only Jesus Christ can wake us. Christ our Light shines within and the unseen is made visible!

Arise to a new dawn. See clearly for the first time. By Christ's light purpose is revealed, power becomes available, and we firmly grasp hope. Christ our Light shows us the many would-be guides sleep-walking on paths of destruction, urging us to follow their trails. No longer groping in the dark, we follow Christ, the Light that leads us out of fear, leads us from death to life. We are no longer outsiders, waiting to be rescued, but become bearers of the Light when we welcome Christ to guide us into all truth.

Turn from death to life, from fear to hope, from darkness to Light. Right now, welcome Jesus Christ as your Light. By His light we will journey together exploring Spiritual Secrets About Suicide.

The Secret of Abounding Power

"You and your husband are good people. You do good work and I appreciate that," Dr. Rich boomed over the high-pitched whine while polishing my teeth. "But God doesn't exist. Look at all the terrible things that happen in this world. And if God does exist, He's powerless, so He isn't God," he mocked. His usual tirade.

Rich was pretty mad about the whole topic of God, which he brought up, and which he was arguing with himself. Even if I wanted to challenge him (and I didn't feel the need), I wasn't in any position to contribute to the conversation!

He could shout with all the lung power of his six-foot-three height, but I knew he would never silence the inner voice that disturbed him because it was God who spoke to Rich's heart. And Rich would never change my mind with human arguments because I had experienced God's supernatural power. And my old friend Rich knew it. God's power was the only explanation for the medical impossibilities that became miraculous realities for me in 1988.

———◆———

In the spring of 1986 I felt I was bursting with color, like our blossoming garden of peace roses, sky blue ageratum, and silvery dusty miller that Ed and I planted around our green ranch home. Hanging a parachute beneath the glass ceiling in our sun room we created a shady summer space. We flung open the patio doors to appreciate our backyard grouping of pitch pines standing watch over goldfish playing in our waterlily pond. On Friday evenings our blender whirred, producing batches of icy drinks. Folks stopped over for a quick catch-up and a welcome to the weekend.

Ed managed the quality control department of a Scotland-based corporation. I had a promising career as a financial planner for a Wall Street firm. We enjoyed work, but looked forward to weekends; especially the Saturday Ed would launch our sailboat, tying it off in our summer slip. Cooking was one of our hobbies. Ed chopped and I sautéed. We moved as well together in the kitchen as we did in life and hosted both intimate dinners and big fun parties with lots of music. With all of the activity, I easily ignored the vague pains occasionally shooting through my hands and feet. But they became more insistent.

One July afternoon, I lounged side-by-side with my aunt on deck chairs aboard a friend's cabin cruiser anchored off Gardiner's Island. I tugged on my red striped sunhat as the breeze picked up, pulling it down firmly on my head. I squinted at the chop on the Long Island Sound, watched foam-crested waves jump in the salt water, heard them splash against the boat. I asked my aunt's opinion about my growing achiness. "Better have it checked out, Honeybun," she advised. Nodding, I shoved that disturbing thought to the back of my mind. I turned my attention to the water and noticed the increasing green tinge, the sign of a storm approaching.

The next Saturday, I drove my mom and sister-in-law, Karen, home from a shopping trip and had an experience I couldn't ignore. Karen chattered in the backseat, making us laugh. As I approached a major intersection notorious for accidents, the traffic light turned red. My foot on the gas pedal would not move. The natural reflex failed. I willed my leg to lift it. No response. I sped toward the intersection. At the last safe moment, my foot shifted to the brake, but it was too weak to depress the pedal. I held my breath, braced my hands against the steering wheel, and forced all of my body weight down. The car stopped. I sat stunned, numb at the thought of the averted disaster.

No one in the car noticed. Gripping the wheel, I didn't say a word about the incident. Mind racing, I stared at the red light, "What will happen when the light turns green?"

But my leg responded normally and we smoothly crossed the ten-lane intersection. When we arrived on the other side, I doubted for a moment. Had the strange occurrence been real? I could not have imagined it. I hadn't heard Karen's joke, but I joined in the laughter. It sounded hollow in my ears.

Monday morning I phoned the doctor. My personal physician recommended a specialist who ordered tests to confirm his suspicion. "Sudden heavy-onset rheumatoid arthritis," the doctor said.

I was diagnosed with an incurable disease.

Rapidly, arthritis grew through my body. Like an oak tree, its hardwood branches spread through my limbs and they became stiff and heavy. My joints felt gnarled, my weakened hands could not grip our sailboat lines. I put away my dancing shoes.

Most of the time I felt worn out and had to sleep a lot, but I didn't wake refreshed. I knew that could be a sign of depression. I asked the rheumatologist, "Does arthritis release a chemical that makes me depressed? Or am I depressed because I have arthritis? Can the medication make me depressed?"

He never answered me. What he did say was, "You can expect to deteriorate to 'bone on bone.' When the cartilage that cushions joints wears away, 'bone on bone' is the result."

We stubbornly refused to accept his dire predictions as the final word

Fixing a stick pin to the lapel of my business suit, Ed said, "You look great, honey." I didn't much like my new "look" that included flat shoes to cope with foot pain. Frowning, I added my inelegant shoes to my mental list of self-criticism. An ever-growing list. I could no longer perform to my standards. Forced to limit my office hours, I saw pity in people's eyes. I overheard two colleagues speculating on their chances of taking over my business accounts.

Home from work one afternoon, my neighbor called to me from over the fence. "Annette, everything okay?" I filled her in and she said, "I knew something was wrong when I didn't hear music coming from your house." True, I could no longer strum my guitar in the backyard, but I would not easily give up the life we had lived.

Proactive, I fought to master arthritis. I read anything I thought would help, took American Arthritis Association workshops, changed my diet, became a swimmer, and practiced relaxation techniques. Still, arthritis progressed rapidly and my capacities diminished.

One night, Ed pulled into a fast food place and went in to buy cheeseburgers for us. Sitting in the parking lot, we joined hands in blessing and Ed dug into the paper bag pulling out salty fries, ketchup, and napkins, setting up our in-car picnic. Our burgers stayed warm in their insulated containers with simple tab inserts to keep them closed. Simple for people without arthritis. I fumbled with the flimsy plastic, becoming more frustrated. Frantic, I tore at the box. Grief fed my desperation. Hot tears erupted from my private hell of raging emotions. My sobs burst through the boundaries I had set, bypassing my insistence on their suppression.

Ed pleaded, "Let me help you!"

"I don't want you to help me," I wailed. "*I want my hands to work!*"

The unopened box tumbled to my feet. Ed reached for me. Gathered into his strong arms, I put my head on his chest and heard his heart breaking.

Swallowing, forcing the monster of fear and anguish back down into the dark cage inside where I kept it chained, I shot the bolt with the enormous strength of my human will, and locked down my dangerous emotions.

I touched Ed's face. He gently caressed mine. "We'll get through this," he promised.

"We will." I nodded. We would, but how?

My mom telephoned, "There is going to be a healing service in Patchogue." With expectation, Ed and I scribbled the date on our calendar. As a child I heard and read about Jesus working miracles and always believed. And when I was sick, Mom took me to church for special prayer. [1]

---

1 The Bible says when we are sick we should call some faithful people and get them to "pray and anoint" us with oil. James 5:14

Church attendance was a part of my life with Ed and we were involved. We brought bags of groceries to families in need. We visited and prayed for the sick, including a man in his twenties with arthritis that resulted in neck surgery. He recuperated in a metal "halo"—a brace that immobilized his head and neck. We knew when we placed our hands on the sick and prayed, God's power was released through us to them.

Ed pushed the door open to the auditorium where the healing service was in progress. A gentleman, he had always held doors for me. But now it was different. I was incapable of opening them for myself. Despite the increased dosage of anti-inflammatory medication, the pain was constant. We arrived late intentionally, because I could no longer sit comfortably for an hour.

"Those who would like prayer, please come forward and form two lines," the usher said.

Ed and I held hands as he walked down the aisle and I maneuvered my way forward, dragging my right leg. I knew what would be expected. The prayer minister would ask me to share my needs. I despised listing my physical problems. The verbalization made them more concrete and I felt less in control. My stomach tightened like a clenched fist, shaking in anger. A churning nausea began and acid burned my throat. I had trained myself to respond with deep breathing, consciously easing the tension.

"Over here, please." The usher directed us to a man in his forties, dressed in a brown tunic, wearing sandals. He asked about our need. I choked on the words.

Ed said, "My wife was diagnosed with rheumatoid arthritis. It started in her feet and keeps spreading through her body. She's in tremendous pain, especially her hands, feet, and right leg."

He bent his head, put his fingers to his chin, and responded thoughtfully, "My friend had that. He was prayed for last spring and over the summer he slowly improved. After a few months, he was completely well."

He put one hand on my shoulder and prayed for my healing, "...in the Name of Jesus. Amen." He was kind and compassionate. It was a nice experience, but I had no apparent change in my physical symptoms. I dragged my leg behind me as we left the church. Ed helped me into the car and drove us home. I was exhausted from the effort.

About ten days later there was a change, but not in my physical body. I saw, with my inner vision, a small flame burning inside me. I was unaware of it in my conscious mind, but my spirit was alert to this interior fire. Some spiritual experiences cannot really be explained. I can compare it with the thumb on my hand. I know it is there, see it daily, but I am not really conscious of it. In the same way, I saw this flame burning within me every day, though not mindful of it. At the same time, a place in me was constantly aware of the continued presence of the interior flame. And I was changed. I had new hope. Soon, the interior change became exterior. Strength began to return.

In the following weeks, a quotation from the Bible continuously ran through my mind as the power of God became evident in my body. "Even now the axe is laid to the root...every tree which does not bear good fruit is cut down and thrown into the fire."[2]

The arthritis that had been so aggressive in my body began to weaken, shrivel, and die back. Like a tree still standing though severed at its root. The "tree of arthritis" had not born any good fruit and had been super-naturally cut down and destroyed through prayer. God's power had done for me what human wisdom said could not be accomplished.

> **God's power had done for me what human wisdom said could not be accomplished.**

Every day my pain eased a bit more and, slowly, function returned. Once again I could tug open the spout on the milk container, twist the lid on the peanut butter jar, and even turn the bolt to unlock the front door! After a period of eight months, I was medication free, and totally, miraculously healed.

---

2 Matthew 3:10

God is the all-powerful King of the supernatural and physical realm, creating and recreating physical realities through His miraculous power. I am the lame who now walks, the disabled one restored, the living proof of His power.

I thank God for doctors who study medicine for years. However, when the doctor says the condition is incurable, inoperable, and deteriorating, I thank God *we* study another book. We are students of the Bible that says Jesus Christ's wounds became our healing.[3]

Maybe you take medication and have been told you will need it for the rest of your life. Maybe you don't like taking medication. I didn't. I was told I would have to increase the dosage throughout my lifetime; I would never be able to discontinue it. That was the medical reality. My father was a pharmacist and he told me, "Don't fight against the medication. Cooperate with it to help yourself." The prescription medication I took helped me function. Thanking God for available helpful medication was part of my journey to wholeness. Many people I have prayed for return to the doctor, have verified improvement, and are told to continue on a lower dose. Some have been advised by their doctor to taper off their medication. Medication, whether increased or reduced, must be handled specifically to keep you safe. Get prayer. Let the doctor examine you, review your medication, and advise you.

3 1Peter 2:24

I don't need medication anymore. God healed me. Do you see a new possibility for your situation?

Maybe you have side effects from your medication. I know that is frustrating. I had side effects, too. I had a dangerous reaction to the first medication my doctor prescribed. I learned how to bless the pills I took. You can do the same in your own words. Here is a suggested prayer to help you. *"In the Name of Jesus I bless this medication. I command this medication to do its job without any negative side effects. Thank you, Jesus."*

Maybe you ache inside. Like your heart is bleeding. Emotional pain can feel black, can feel endless. Our living God calls us out of darkness into His marvelous light. God says without knowledge people perish. You must not perish through lies and false teaching. It is the knowledge of Jesus Christ's true loving nature that saves. Jesus Christ loves you with endless extravagance. His power is boundless. Stop the lies by embracing the truth about God and accessing His saving power.

Maybe you are planning your own funeral. I can relate to those feelings. Arthritis kills people. Hurtling toward a disastrous end, I was preparing our home for Ed's future without me. I already felt like the living dead. But God changed the trajectory of my life. And God can do that for you.

Spiritual truths are not found in every pulpit, in every white lab coat, or at every news anchor desk. However, spiritual truth is available to all who seek it wholeheartedly. The quest for spiritual truth demands an investment of time and energy, but it is worth pursuing. Once discovered, it never changes.

When I was in high school, we memorized a photosynthesis formula that was changed when scientists found it incorrect. We were misinformed by our teacher and mistaken researchers. Medical science is also changing, acknowledging the whole person is body, mind, and spirit. Many recognize spiritual care is necessary to health.

Spiritual truth is available to all who seek it wholeheartedly.

I made every effort to surround myself with physicians that believed life was much more than could be examined through a microscope. Healing demands an integrated approach.

My primary care physician always encouraged me to expect God's intervention. I have spoken to medical doctors about positive reversals in a patient's health who say, "It's a miracle. I've seen those before." However, sometimes miracles are denied even when medically confirmed. As in the case of Ferdinand.

Ed and I noticed Ferdinand in Amontada, Brazil. The skinny pre-teen with dark curly-hair snuck up on an unsuspecting boy in the congregation, punched him hard in the arm, and then ran wild through the church as though daring the boy to catch him. The musicians led the song and our host whispered to me, "That boy needs prayer. His birth mother had measles while he was in her womb. He was born deaf and mute. That's his adoptive mother," he said pointing out a heavyset lady, hair pulled back in a ponytail, praying with her eyes closed. "Ferdinand communicates by lip reading. He needs prayer." I passed the message to Ed and while the music continued, Ed approached Ferdinand. Through simple signs, Ed asked if he could pray for him and the boy nodded. I watched Ed place his hands on the boy. A few minutes later, Ed snapped his fingers next to the boy's ear. Ferdinand signaled thumbs up. Ed snapped his fingers near the other ear. Again, thumbs up.

Our host translated the news to Ferdinand's adoptive mother. Her were eyes closed in prayer, she had not seen Ed approach or pray for her boy. She turned Ferdinand to face her and in Portuguese said, "Say Mama."

He looked into her eyes and for the first time said, "Mama!"

She pulled Ferdinand into her arms and covered her face with one hand as tears coursed down her cheeks. She brought him to our next Bridge for Peace healing prayer ministry in an auditorium. Ferdinand complained that the music was too loud!

Four years later, we saw Ferdinand again. The tall young man gently held his younger brother in his arms. Talking to his adoptive mother through a translator, I learned the doctor said he had 75% hearing in what had been totally deaf ears. However, the doctor said Ferdinand had lost so many years of hearing, that even though he could now speak, he would never speak well. And they believed him.

I was angry. No doctor, medicine or surgery had healed Ferdinand's hearing. God healed him. The power of God that caused deaf Fedinand to hear, that gave the mute boy a voice, could also give him intelligible speech. That is only logical. Reject the lie that God is powerless or inadequate. I don't know how God has worked in that doctor's life, but I do know that as God continually demonstrates His loving power, people change their minds about Him.

After many years, my friend Dr. Rich, who sneered at the existence of God and denied His power, had a change of heart. He told me, "I pray to God every night." He found God through two ordeals with cancer. At his request, Ed and I prayed both with him and for him. Though he came through each sickness, he told me he didn't love God because He cured him or didn't cure him. He loved God because he came to know God's love and life-giving power. I found many share Dr. Rich's story.

I have interviewed people from different age groups and nationalities tormented by depression and suicide, some of whom had been hospitalized in psychiatric units. I asked if they would be willing to tell me their stories. I planned only to listen,

...depression lessened and their suicidal thoughts decreased when they invited Jesus Christ to live in them.

not to prompt or lead. The few questions I did ask were to clarify what I did not understand. I did not expect to draw conclusions, but to increase my knowledge of people's experience with suicidal thoughts. As their stories unfolded, I was amazed to see a pattern. Often I heard, "I didn't believe in God..." or "I didn't know God could..." Either God's existence or God's power was always mentioned. Many people had three major turning points in common.

The first step I identified was their adult decision for Christ. Many said their depression lessened and their suicidal thoughts decreased when they invited Jesus Christ to live in them and take charge of their lives. It is not a failure to remain on medication, but those who discussed their medications with me said they now take fewer medications, lower dosages or no medication at all.

Some had a period of retaliation when tormenting thoughts increased, but then the voice lost power, became muffled. In a later chapter, I will discuss this common phenomenon.

You can make a choice now to take step one in creating a new life. Pray and ask Jesus Christ to stop the lies you believed about God, about yourself, about your future. You can ask Jesus Christ to save you from all destruction and show you the meaning of your life. If you have already committed yourself to Jesus Christ, this is an opportunity to renew your pledge. God wants you to live. Promise to live for him.

——◆——

God, You show Yourself to us in miracles. In the miraculous healing of arthritis and in restoring hearing to deaf ears, You do what no other can do. You invite us to glimpse Your beauty—Your immeasurability—in flaming clouds of sunset reaching from the horizon and spreading over us in sapphire sky. You patiently wait through our anger and rejection; loving us, even those who, like Dr. Rich, argue against Your existence. You stay close when we are frustrated with senseless violence in the world and when, in our thoughts, we do violence to ourselves. When we ask, "How will I get through this?" You invite us to find the answer in You. You ask us to make a decision to take hold of Your hand and put our lives in it. You promise us hope, a future, a purposeful life through Your son Jesus Christ. You ask us to call on the Name of Jesus and experience boundless power that heals. You who created life reveal the meaning of life.

Tricked in the past by lies, today we invite You to free us. We know You exist and we call on Your help. You are able to work in mental illness, emotional bondage, and physical sickness. You are not bound by medical diagnoses, dire prognoses or any negative word that has been spoken over us by parents, teachers, or any other authority figures in our lives. We know You have power and so we have hope. We receive Your promise that no weapon formed to destroy us will succeed. We receive Your invitation to become alive and abounding in You.

THE SECRET of the BLOOD

EMERGENCY
BLOOD
SHORTAGE
DONATE BLOOD
NOW!
PEOPLE
CAN'T LIVE
WITHOUT IT

Rushing into the locker room at the gym I came around the corner and stopped, confronted by the poster on the wall. The plain truth simply put. Our physical bodies cannot survive without blood. But life is more than the needs and operation of our physical bodies!

The sounds of exquisite music cause us to soar. The intrigues of the unknown lead us to explore. These experiences and longings are not born of the physical body. Mysterious realms within us give birth to imaginative thoughts and hidden emotions that cannot be detected by diagnostic instrumentation. These unobservable places need the life supplied by the Blood of Jesus. Our authentic selves, free and vibrant, are sustained through Christ's life-giving Blood. Jesus Christ freely donated an unending supply of His Blood for us so we may truly live.

———◆———

The warm roll-down-the-car-window day in April coaxed white magnolias and crimson tulips to blossom. Beginning a new week, beginning a new life miraculously free of arthritis, I drove home from work singing loudly in my Honda. One more corner, around the horseshoe turn, and home. My speedometer read 50, the limit for the four lane road. Green light ahead. A Hyundai waited at the light to turn and cross traffic. I was close enough to see the blonde woman at the wheel, when she gunned her engine and sped out in front of me.

Too late, too late…

I jammed on the brakes, my tires screeched. I knew I couldn't stop in time. No oncoming traffic. I clutched the wheel, swerved into the oncoming traffic lane, and braced for impact. The sickening sound of the head-on collision shuddered through me. I jerked forward, slammed back into the seat. The car rocked and settled into the silence of aftermath.

A couple of passenger cars pulled to the side of the road. A man rushed to my window, "Are you okay?"

I nodded.

"I saw the whole thing. There was nothing you could do. I'll testify." He wrote as he talked. "Here's my number. Are you sure you're okay? "

Sirens. Spinning red lights. Police. An ambulance raced onto the scene, but I would not be getting into it. I vividly recalled 1971.

Ed and I had been driving northbound on the Rhode Island Interstate when a drunk driver careened south in the same lane. Head-on collision. We had both been hospitalized. I had a long recovery.

Now, as I sat shaking in my smashed-up Honda, I thought, "No one is calling Ed from the hospital to tell him I've been in a car accident." I couldn't control what had just happened, but I would control how he heard about it.

The tow truck charged onto the scene with piercing high-pitched bleeping and flashing yellow lights. The acrid exhaust poured through my window as the driver maneuvered to remove the wrecked vehicle. My car was drivable and I had two miles to go. Unable to convince me to get in the ambulance, the policeman escorted me home.

Pulling into the driveway, I stepped out of the car and nearly fell back against it. For a moment, my spine failed to support me. Gathering strength and determination, I made it to the front door while running through a mental list of what I could do to help myself. Applying every home remedy I could find in the medicine cabinet, I phoned Ed and explained what happened. "I'm okay, really."

"I'm coming right home."

"Be careful on the road." I grimaced as I said it. "Love you."

About half an hour later he barreled into the bedroom, anxiety etching lines in his face.

"I'm okay, don't worry."

"You don't look okay."

The next morning, I slowly climbed out of bed. Sounds became distant and the room went black. I came to in Ed's arms. The ambulance was on its way. The EMTs hoisted me on the stretcher and delivered me to the hospital. My diagnosis included concussion, seizures, skeletal system and nerve damage, internal organs affected, and more. The medical answer was drugs and physical therapy.

Immobilized by pain, I lay in bed consumed by the immediate demands of my condition and worried about the return of arthritis. I thought about Terry, a man I knew who became arthritic from a misstep off a curb. His hands gnarled and useless, he was crippled by arthritis and in a wheelchair. I just had another major trauma. In the prior eighteen months of managing arthritis, I had to keep moving or stiffness worsened. What would happen now that I was bedridden?

I needed twenty-four hour assistance for over three months. Woozy all of the time, I fought to stay conscious. Ed took time off from work. Friends, family, and church family sat with me and shuttled me to appointments.

Once again, I heard a familiar prognosis, "Incurable. Inoperable. Deteriorating."

Sophisticated tests uncovered more medical problems. Specialists disagreed about treatment. Adding to our confusion, they complained to us about prescriptions ordered by other doctors saying, "No patient of mine takes this medication!" Or, "I wouldn't use any drug that hadn't been in the field ten years." Or "This drug is contraindicated for concussion patients!"

My personal physician advised against prescribed painkillers. He said, "You'll become an addict like other back patients."

I wouldn't touch painkillers after his advice, or the muscle relaxers that gave me negative side effects. At night I'd crawl out of bed and lay on the floor rolling side to side with pain.

The orthopedic surgeon repeated himself saying, "I don't know what to do with you. Look at these x-rays! The worst whiplash I've ever seen, but you are not a candidate for surgery. I think you should go back in the hospital for traction." Unconvinced it would be helpful, I refused.

At my appointment with Judy, the physical therapist employed by the orthopedic surgeon, she worked through the soles of my feet. Every other part of my body was untouchable because of pain.

One morning, she glanced around the therapy room, pulled the privacy curtain, leaned close and whispered, "You'll never get better if you stay here."

Because I was not progressing, she recommended a physical therapist who could educate Ed and me in alternative modalities.

When my brain healed enough, I invested myself in studying the Bible, Christian healing, and books by medical pioneers of the '90s, including Dr. Jean Barral, Dr. Meir Schneider and Dr. John Upledger—innovative doctors who considered the spiritual aspect of human beings in their practice.

Some answers came through a Manhattan physician who specialized in the new field of psychoneuroimmunology, but we still had many questions. Our search for help took us to a rehab center in Florida and a physician in France. I arrived in the Paris airport in a wheelchair for the appointment with a doctor who was an author and professor at the University of Paris. Within moments of examining me, he asked if I had vertigo, explained the cause, and taught Ed to help me. After months of very few answers about my condition, in a few moments he became a trusted advisor.

These brilliant doctors relieved some of my

symptoms and we were encouraged to persevere, but they couldn't offer much hope of recovery from my incapacitating problems.

I continued to seek prayer, participated in healing services and prayer groups. I couldn't sit up for long, so I lay on the floor in the back of churches or on the sofa in home prayer groups.

One morning, I gingerly lowered myself onto the sofa in our sun room. The self-help book I was reading suggested a collage exercise. Armed with scissors and magazines, I was ready to follow the instructions. Cutting and pasting was a slow process, and sometime later I assessed my finished work. My throat tightened. The pictures I had arranged on the poster board clearly showed a battle between good and evil. The collage depicted dark spirits striving to gain control while angels guarded me.

I had no conscious realization of the fight, but God put a capacity in us to touch the spiritual world, to see the invisible. The creative act of placing pictures in harmonious positions quieted the dominance of my mind and gave space for my God-given spirit to express itself on art paper. My spirit communicated with my mind through the creative work. The collage became a window into my awareness of an otherworldly struggle.

> **God put a capacity in us to touch the spiritual world.**

I had fed my spirit by Bible reading and prayer, and my spirit wanted to give voice to the spiritual realities it understood. My God-given aptitude to recognize spiritual truth could only help me if I quieted the self-talk and paid attention.

I recognized the familiar insistence of the firm "inner tug" that had guided me at different times in my life. Alerted to what I had come to know as the voice of the Holy Spirit, I sensed, "This is important, pay attention!"

The Holy Spirit is not a bully. I could choose to turn toward the Holy Spirit's prompting or opt to turn away and distract myself. The Holy Spirit does not compel us to listen to God's wisdom. Even if I had disregarded the interior nudge of the Holy Spirit (which I was not inclined to do) I may not have been able to ignore the growing awareness of an unseen hostile presence. I stilled myself to hear God's voice. I stayed with the feeling.

Gradually, as though awakening from a dream, I remembered what I had learned about the spiritual battle between evil and humanity as explained in the first book of the Bible, Genesis. God's Word describes it as the hostility, the war, the enmity between humankind and demonic forces. I knew demons existed, acted through us, and influenced our world, but that truth had become a very small part of my big picture. An appreciator by nature, I had been focused on the blessings of my marriage, family, and friends, our beautiful home, church involvement, and our growing careers. Though I understood that the spiritual battle continued to rage, it had not been in the forefront of my mind. That is, not until now.

Unnerved, I called Pastor Eric, a friend for nearly twenty years and a trusted counsellor. "Pastor, I know it sounds strange, but I feel some kind of evil presence is trying to influence me."

He spoke in a matter-of-fact way and reassured me, made my experience feel normal. "Read 1John 4 in the Bible," he advised.

"Thanks Pastor."

Still flustered, I turned to the Gospel of John by mistake, instead of 1John, which is a different book in the Bible. Because I was in the wrong place, I didn't see any relevance in the passage.

A disquieting sense of a dark presence continued. I felt an insistence to reach out for help. I phoned a family member for prayer and he gave me the number for his pastor.

On the phone, I introduced myself to the pastor and plunged into my story speaking calmly with my professional voice. "I have a sense of the presence of dark spirits." I sounded a little crazy even to myself. "I was wondering if you could give me any advice?"

"Well, call on the Name of Jesus," he said. He sounded bored, like he was reading the newspaper while talking to me.

"I have a bit of an unusual situation." I continued, "I have had a couple of serious car accidents and have just been miraculously cured by Jesus from a debilitating disease…" Something I said caused him to snap to attention. I felt the shift over the phone. His voice became serious. "Listen, pray the covering of the Blood of Jesus over yourself."

> "…pray the covering of the Blood of Jesus over yourself."

I imagined my head covered in blood. Not a good image.

I thought, *This conversation is over.* He attempted to keep me on the line, but I thanked him for his time, and hung up.

In 1971, I had been thrown through the car windshield. I woke up in emergency as the surgeon was tying off the last of over one hundred stitches in my head. When I was released from the hospital, the plastic surgeon advised me to swab the wound three times daily with hydrogen peroxide. Dried blood clung to the stitches in the first weeks of treating the injury. The pastor's suggestion to cover myself with Blood recalled the dried blood on my forehead.

The pastor's strange words were repulsive. Why would I cover myself with the Blood of Jesus?

Reaching for my Bible again, I paged through and found 1John 4, the correct scripture passage Pastor Eric recommended. It began, "Dear friends, do not believe every spirit, but test the spirits to determine if they are from God…"[1] This was perfect for my situation!

"By this you know the Spirit of God: Every spirit that confesses Jesus as the Christ who has come in the flesh is from God, but every spirit that does not confess Jesus is not from God…" That was easy for me to understand. I remembered my friend Dr. Rich who said there is no God. He had been blinded by demonic spirits who kept him from seeing the truth.

Verse 4 began, "You young people…" I identified myself in the group of 'young people' John was addressing and felt he was writing his letter directly to me.

"…I have written you because you are strong—the Word of God remains in you, and you have overcome the evil one. You…have conquered them (ungodly spirits) because the One who is in you is greater than the one who is in the world."

God is greater than evil spirits.

The words found a home in me. I thought, *I am strong. I am from God. I have overcome evil spirits. I have conquered evil spirits. God is greater than evil spirits.* Reading and repeating these truths grounded me. I was not a victim. I was an overcomer, a conqueror through Christ!

When I sensed the presence of evil spirits I had

---

1 1John 4:1

become vulnerable to fear of evil spirits because of my circumstances. I was in pain, my emotions were battered, and I was uncertain of the future with my career on hold, my economic strength gone. The scripture reminded me who I was.

I had no reason to fear evil spirits. I belonged to all-powerful God.

Occasionally, the pastor's words about the Blood of Jesus came to mind, maybe because I had a strong emotional reaction to them. The memory didn't fade and strangely enough my understanding of the Blood of Jesus began to deepen.

As a child I was taught about Jesus's crucifixion and His Blood shed for the forgiveness of my sins because He loved me. I knew through Jesus Christ we have eternal life in heaven when we love Him. Every Sunday for years I had heard the scripture, "For this is My Blood, the Blood of the new and eternal covenant which will be poured out for you and for many for the forgiveness of sins." [2] I had memorized Jesus's words about His Blood, but what did they mean?

I realized I had an unusual viewpoint on blood since childhood.

I was eleven years old, sitting on the cement stoop in front of our home, examining my right knee. Playing with the neighborhood kids, I'd fallen on the sidewalk and scraped the flesh off of my

---

2 Matt 26:28, Mark 14:24

knee. It really stung! I was pleased to see blood ooze out, mixed with bits of sand grains.

I wasn't afraid of blood. I had been told blood cleanses wounds. That was great, since we knew dirty cuts were trouble! We knew about tetanus shots! So, when blood trickled out, I thought *good*. I told other bleeding kids, "Don't worry. The blood is good! It is cleaning the cut!"

I was thinking about the parallels between our human blood and the Blood of Jesus as I drove to meet my friend Dr. Mary, a pediatric physician. I thought of our human woundedness and the remedy for our mental and emotional pain. Out loud in the car I said, "The Blood of Jesus heals our wounds." I repeated it a couple of times and went on to say, "The Blood of Jesus heals our wounded relationship with God."

I met Mary in the parking lot. We strolled across the duck pond bridge and I asked about her son. I hadn't seen him in years. "What is he doing now?"

"He teaches doctors and nurses about wound care." Mary launched into an enthusiastic description of her own medical training in wound care, the packing of wounds for diabetic patients, and the wonders of negative pressure in stimulating the healing of wounds. "Chronic wounds are becoming more prevalent and more difficult to treat."

I thought, *This is not a coincidence.* I mentioned to Mary, "I was just thinking about the importance of blood in healing wounds as I drove here."

"Oh, I love what blood does! Yes! People think blood is just red blood cells, but the white blood cells in blood are so important…" Mary quickly outlined for me the crucial role blood plays in healing wounds. "When you see how nature works, it makes you want to fall down and worship God. If only we would take the time to pay attention and get it. You know that verse in Romans? The one that says something like, 'He is seen in nature, in what He has created.'[3] If we would only open our eyes and see!"

> **Blood plays a crucial role in healing wounds.**

This is my recap of the complex activity of the blood. It cleans, protects, and nurtures the wound. Astonishingly, blood "directs" the healing process. Specialized blood cells rush to the site of physical wounds and assault bacteria or viruses with diverse specialized weapons which we observe as healthy inflammation. The area may be tender during this phase. Inflammation ends when the blood assesses the wound bed is clean and ready for healing. Then the blood oversees the repair process! It supplies the right balance of oxygen for wound healing. Too much or too little and the wound won't heal correctly.

---

3 Romans 1:20 For since the creation of the world His invisible attributes—His eternal power and divine nature—have been clearly seen, because they are understood through what has been made. So people are without excuse.

Blood disposes of dead tissue, brings new life, and regenerates. Blood continues to strengthen the new tissue. Thank God for blood!

"Mary, I was thinking that what our physical blood does is exactly what the Blood of Jesus does. The Blood of Jesus supernaturally penetrates our wounds. The festering sores in our hearts, our traumatic memories, our broken relationship with God—every wound! The natural order of how our human blood heals our wounds mirrors what the Blood of Jesus does for us."

"That's right! That's it!" she affirmed.

First Christ's Blood cleanses us, purifies us, washes away everything unclean. Then Jesus's Blood tends the festering sores in our hearts and the traumatic memories in us. These wounds may seem sore and fresh through the process, but the Blood is at work, thoroughly removing all unhealthy grief and anger, all unforgiveness. Having cleaned out all of that dead, toxic mess, the Blood begins to make us whole, setting our lives in divine order, all the time protecting us from further injury. The Blood of Jesus nurtures us. It builds something new in our lives. It strengthens us on a daily basis. The

> **Christ's Blood cleanses us, purifies us, washes away everything unclean.**

41

Blood of Jesus restores our relationship to God by directing and ordering everything.

The pastor on the telephone meant, *Call on the Blood of Jesus. It is good. It will cleanse you from the influence of filthy evil spirits.* But I didn't understand. I found the whole idea of applying blood gruesome. Now I know praying to be "covered in the Blood of Jesus" is crucial in the battle against all evil, including suicide.

Sharon discovered power in the Blood of Jesus to help her to heal. She had planned her own death and obtained the means more than once. She had been in several psychiatric hospitals. "When I started to understand what the Blood of Jesus meant it changed things. I could apply the Blood of Jesus myself whenever I was hurting." Diane found that the Blood of Jesus "works." "Suicidal thoughts kept coming, but I didn't feel I had to do what they said." She began to resist them with the Blood of Jesus. "There is power there in the Blood of Jesus. I can't explain it, but it is real."

> "There is power there in the Blood of Jesus. I can't explain it, but it is real."

Every one of us is invited to apply the Blood of Jesus for the healing of our minds. Jesus already gave His Blood for your healing. There is no shortage. You can receive His Blood freely and apply it anytime you feel a need. The following prayer is a guide. You can pray this to apply the Blood of Jesus to your mind or for someone else.

———◆———

Jesus Christ, thank You that You have made Your own Blood freely available to us. I do not understand everything about Your supernatural power or the mystery of Your cross, but I know You want me to apply Your Blood to my mind to deliver me from the power of tormenting thoughts. Your Blood was poured out for me when You were crucified. Supernaturally, Your Blood is available to me in this present moment. In Your Name Jesus, I apply Your Blood to my mind through prayer right now. I know this pleases You, and the saints and angels in heaven rejoice.

Thank You, Jesus, for penetrating my mind, my memory, my woundedness, and cleansing me from ungodly thoughts.

Thank You for protecting me and nurturing me through the healing process that begins right now. I invite Your Blood into my woundedness to expose any unforgiveness or ungodly thoughts that have lodged like bad bacteria, causing festering infection and continual pain. Thank You for Your power, through which I forgive all who have hurt me, living or dead. I am grateful that You forgive me whenever I ask. Thank You that through Your power, right now, I can forgive myself.

You lead me step by step through transformation. I know You love and care for me. Though I may feel sensitive and vulnerable as You work within me, You will nurture me, and show me how to nurture myself. Thank You for overseeing the entire healing process.

You guide me into my life's purpose. I receive wisdom from You to make right choices for my life. I receive Your strength to walk in the good paths You show me. Thank You for bringing Your healthy balance into my life, the right amounts of rest, recreation, and work, the right amounts of food and prayer. Teach me how to relate to others in healthy relationships.

Thank You for directing all of my medical care. I pray for all those in the healthcare profession that I have already met. I pray You will send me Your pick to meet my medical needs.

I pray for those You have sent and will send to help me grow spiritually. Send me Your teachers Lord! Thank You, Lord, as You continue to strengthen me in all the details of my life. Thank You, Jesus Christ, for healing me through Your Blood.

THE SECRET of DELIVERANCE

Dr. Poland, former Prevention Division Director of the American Association of Suicidology, clicked to another slide in his presentation on suicide prevention, intervention, and postvention. I was seated in the Marriott Hotel ballroom among two hundred participants hoping to learn how to better help people in our community. Twice, Dr. Poland mentioned the importance of church involvement in the prevention of suicide. My research showed the World Health Organization promoted the participation of spiritual and religious leaders in suicide prevention. A new slide appeared entitled "More Protective Factors." The fifth bullet point listed "religiosity."

Followers of Jesus Christ are equipped to help in a specialized area of spiritual care. When depression and suicidal thoughts fall into the category of demonic influence, trained Christians know how to carry out the intervention plan Jesus Christ detailed in the Gospels.

Christ's church knows demons are real. Jesus Christ and His disciples delivered people harassed by evil spirits.[1] Jesus Christ commanded His followers to do the same.[2] The Holy Spirit equips us to obey Christ's directive.

Mental health associations say that most of the population has experienced sad feelings associated with a life event, perhaps an unexpected loss, called "situational" depression.

When arthritis was active in my body I slept many hours, a classic symptom of depression. I asked the rheumatologist if the medication I took caused depression. Or did arthritis cause exhaustion, in which case extra rest was a "healthy" response in my self-care plan. If it was not a side effect of my medication and if it was not an expected physiological change due to arthritis, then I needed a strategy to deal with depression as a result of my psychological and emotional pain. I needed information, because I did not know if I was "depressed" or not.

At a physical therapy session after my second car accident, I remember talking to the therapist. "I think I'm a little depressed." He said, "I think with what you've been through you wouldn't be normal if you weren't depressed."

1 Mark 3:14 – 15, 6,7, 12-13.
2 Mark 3:15-18

We grapple with life. We get hurt. We heal. We go on. Sadness, grief, and anger are healthy responses to some of life's challenges. Frustrations can present opportunities for transformation. Patience, wisdom, and perseverance increase as we grow and reevaluate. We develop new strategies to cope.

The Anxiety and Depression Association of America describes anxious and sad feelings as a normal reaction to some of life's stressors. They also describe three main types of depressive disorders and suggest treatments. Depression can have biological components that need to be addressed through medical treatment, but other factors may be involved.

Christian teaching tells us demonic spirits can cause depression. I learned about the demonic spirit of depression first-hand while on mission in Jamaica, West Indies in 2000.

Christian teaching tells us demonic spirits can cause depression.

Our mission team ministered in the cathedral in Brownstown, Jamaica where, despite the heat, people pumped their arms in the air glorifying God. They sang as the musicians played and drowned out the familiar night sounds of blaring rap music, howling dogs, and the shrieking sirens of emergency vehicles.

The team of Bridge for Peace missionaries served with God's love. God touched and healed many people.

I especially remember a woman who had knee problems. She whispered to me, "Don't tell anyone, I'm a doctor." She received prayer and walked out healed that night.

A young man stood outside the cathedral door and wouldn't come in. He watched a woman demonstrate the limitation of her frozen shoulder as she tried to raise her arm, pain etching her face. It barely came up halfway. After the Bridge for Peace team prayed, she raised her arm over her head, pain-free. Then the young man came in to receive prayer in the Name of Jesus.

People testified to what God was doing and the service was incredible. I praised God that night. But meanwhile, one thought repeated through my mind: *When this mission is over, I'm pulling the plug.*

In the prior twelve years, since founding Bridge for Peace, Ed and I had ministered to people from India, Indonesia, Switzerland, and other nations in our home. We operated our office from our attic and held prayer meetings there, too. One Kenyan brother pulled out the sofa bed after a prayer meeting and said: "I love this place. It's an office by day, a church at night, and then it becomes a hotel."

We helped Christian churches in the USA by offering workshops and weekends of healing and we launched outreaches in remote areas of other nations. We led short term mission teams, prayed with Christians in Pakistan, met with members of China's underground church, and assisted in Africa.

By this point in my life I had weathered lots of personal suffering and lots of disillusionment, but still life was a joyful adventure, the future full of promise. We had numerous satisfying worldwide friendships. While Ed and I had challenges, we also had amazing times when God revealed His glory to us. Sometimes, we stayed up late into the night marveling at God's overwhelming revelation of His unfathomable magnificence.

Each morning I prayed and felt God's Presence. I served God daily, counseled people, prayed for the sick, served food to the hungry on the streets, and tended endless administrative details. This was my life. I still coped with physical effects of the accidents, but God was healing me daily and through my long recuperation, arthritis never returned! I was grateful, blessings abounded, but a new shadow of oppression cast its darkness over the future.

I couldn't name a specific incident that triggered my mood. Nothing in daily life had changed, but I had changed. It was strange to feel my heart heavy in my chest, as if unshed tears weighed it down.

One afternoon I sifted through paperwork in our Bridge for Peace office. The atmosphere hummed with contentment—a few volunteers on computers, others on the phones. Unexpectedly, I felt tears come to my eyes.

I went to the window and looked out at pink blossoms on the apple trees. I made a mindless comment about the beautiful buds, while secretly wiping tears from my cheeks. The brilliant blue sky and wispy white clouds made me feel even sadder.

Muttering something, I fled the room. I was confused. I didn't understand myself. *I must be tired,* I told myself, *I just need a break.* In answer to my unspoken prayer, a friend gave us a week in her Florida condo.

We flew down from New York, excited and happy. Ed unlocked the door to our vacation apartment. Sunshine streamed through sliding glass doors and splashed across the white-carpeted living room adjacent to the kitchen. One of the bedrooms had a Jacuzzi tub, a perfect environment for relaxation.

The next day I rose early and padded into the spare bedroom where my Bible and notebook waited. I prayed. I read the Bible. Finally, I wrote in my journal.

"Lord, I don't know what is wrong with me, probably I just need rest and I'll be recharged and ready to serve again." I wrote for three pages and ended with, "Is this a pancake day, Lord?"

I reread my last entry, my forehead wrinkling. A pancake day? We used to look forward to pancakes on weekends—buttermilk, blueberry, chocolate chip. But now we avoided all those breakfast carbs that made us groggy.

I found Ed relaxing on the sofa, soft classical music playing and golden morning light spilling into the room. He said, "I found this pancake place in the paper. Would you like to go for breakfast?"

"That's amazing!" I replied. I told him what I'd written in my journal.

"Let's go," he said, reaching for the phone to get directions.

A man welcomed us as we arrived and seated us in a booth. I took in the striped beige and burgundy wallpaper, pictures of country scenes, and the aroma of sausage. The waiter brought menus, but I didn't have much appetite. I knew it was time to try to express to Ed my unexplainable emotions and the conclusions I had come to.

Ed ordered for us and the waiter brought our black coffees in white mugs. Toying with the mug, I began. "Honey, I don't understand what is happening inside of me, but…" Again, without knowing why, I felt tears well up in my eyes. "I don't think I can keep going in ministry. It's too hard. I keep hearing in my head *pull the plug.*"

Bit by bit, I started to share my struggles and discouragements. There wasn't any new information; we had lived the ministry hand-in-hand. There were no secrets. Ed knew what the ministry cost us. It was my strength to withstand challenges that had changed. Our daily routine that demanded flexibility and creativity now seemed overwhelming.

"Maybe it is just a cumulative effect. I don't know. I just don't want to go on like this. I want to pull the plug on leading teams and training people. Can't we simplify it all? Just go off, the two of us, and minister to people in need as we meet them?" I asked.

Our server arrived with two small glasses of orange juice and placed them on the mica table in front of us. "Thank you," we said in unison.

"Oh, you are very welcome," he said politely. But he wasn't done. He looked into my face for a moment and smiled. I noticed how his dark skin formed deep creases around his brown eyes, as if he smiled often. A white apron covered his husky form. His name pin read "Yogi."

"The light shines brighter even as the times get darker," Yogi said. "People ask me, 'Why are you so happy? Don't you have any problems?' Sure I have problems; you can't get through this life without trouble. But I know what to do with my problems. I take them to God! I take them to the throne room of the Lord and I leave them at Jesus Christ's feet." His voice rose to a crescendo as he said, "Yes, the light shines brighter even as the times get darker."

Then he added, "I'll be right back with your pancakes." He turned and walked away.

Ed and I looked at each other. In that one instant I was totally changed.

I grinned at Ed, a genuine smile. "It's over," I said.

"It's gone! The heavy feeling, the discouragement—it's gone!" I felt like laughing. In fact, I did laugh!

We knew without a doubt that the Lord had sent Yogi! When Yogi returned with our pancakes, I told him we were in ministry, but I was ready to quit. "My husband didn't know how I felt, we were discussing my feelings for the first time when you came over and started speaking to us about God."

"The moment I saw you, I knew I had to speak to you, but the Lord said it wasn't time yet," Yogi said.

I slathered my pancakes with butter and maple syrup. Then I asked for hash browns and rye toast to go with the bacon Ed already ordered. The darkness was gone. The heaviness in me, the sudden unexplained teary moments that came out of nowhere, all left in that moment through the ministry of a Christian man in a pancake house.

The evil spirit tried to destroy Bridge for Peace ministry of healing to the nations through me. The evil spirit attached itself to me in Jamaica, West Indies. I didn't have thoughts that depressed me—wasn't reviewing situations or feeling bad about particular events. I just felt an overwhelming sadness, a heaviness. I then looked for a reason that I felt overwhelmed and figured that it had to be my daily life. I concluded, "This is too hard." Even though it had not been too hard before.

My brief, intense experience gave me insight into the terrible suffering people can go through, whether from an evil spirit, chemical imbalance, traumatic events, or a combination of these or other causes for depression. Unlike twice before—in the instance of arthritis and the aftermath of the two accidents—I didn't have to ask any professional if I was depressed. The outcome proved to me that I had been oppressed by a spirit of depression.

When Yogi spoke, the power of truth instantly delivered me from the evil spirit. I never again experienced any emotion that even remotely resembled that episode. I'm in the same ministry, doing the same things (with more wisdom in how to help people through Jesus Christ), and loving it.

Evil spirits cannot be medicated, they must be cast out.

Evil spirits cannot be medicated, they must be cast out. Medication that slows the mind down might reduce the effect of suggestions made by an evil spirit of depression. I don't have experience in that realm, since I have never taken medication for depression. And depression can have different root causes. But when it is caused by a spirit of depression, the power of deliverance through Jesus Christ is needed.

A mother told me the story of her son. "He got involved with troubled people, with drugs, and other criminal offenses. Sometimes he becomes angry and depressed saying, 'darkness pulls him down.' The dark episodes are occasional and when he is inappropriate, he apologizes." She was frightened by his behaviors and asked, "Is he possessed?"

"No," I responded. Demonic influence is not possession. Possession is the total control of an evil spirit over a human personality. Possession is a serious extraordinary diabolical action consisting of taking possession of the body of a person and acting through the person. Human beings were not created to be puppets of the enemy. God created us to be in partnership with Him, to release His power into this world.

Consider the facts of my pancake story from another angle. Yogi is a waiter, that's what he does. And by his own admission, he has problems. Still, God used him to free me from a spirit of depression. What does that say for every servant of God? Jesus Christ wants to use us to set people free.

The power of deliverance from spirits of darkness comes from the Holy Spirit through Jesus Christ.

I prayed for a beautiful blonde-haired woman in her forties. Joanna couldn't control her tears. Her eyelids were swollen, her eyes bloodshot, her face flushed. She had been in and out of psychiatric institutions, depressed, and mostly unable to get out of her bed. She couldn't care for herself or her family. A friend brought her

Deliverance from spirits of darkness comes from Jesus Christ.

for ministry at a Bridge for Peace event on their way to the psychiatric hospital.

She was obviously distraught. Her courage to come for prayer, even though she was in such tremendous emotional pain, blessed me. I prayed for her immediately.

I explained, "Joanna, you need the equipping power of the Holy Spirit to fight your battle, which is also spiritual. Have you been baptized in the Holy Spirit?"

She nodded, wiping tears from her face.

"Not baptized as a baby, but as an adult. Making an adult decision to serve Jesus Christ and asking for Jesus Christ to send you the Holy Spirit?"

Joanna shook her head no. She had been a Christian for many years, but had no familiarity with the baptism of the Holy Spirit.

I explained how Jesus appeared to His apostles after He died and was resurrected.[3] "These disciples of His, these followers, had been with him daily, had seen Him heal people, and healed people themselves as He had taught them to do. When Jesus's students went out to minister to people Jesus said, 'I saw Satan fall like lightning.'[4] His students were powerhouses in setting people free!

"Still, Jesus told them they were not ready. They-

---

3 Acts 1:3-5
4 Luke 10:18

were not equipped. He told them to wait in the upper room until the Holy Spirit came to them."[5]

As my eyes stayed locked on hers, I saw her confusion cloud her dilated pupils. I knew she was trying to follow me. I prayed the Holy Spirit would make plain to her what she needed to know.

"We can imagine that they didn't really understand what Jesus was talking about. But, they prayed and waited for the Holy Spirit as Jesus had told them. When the Holy Spirit came on them the Bible says He came like a mighty wind and like flames of fire on each one! They lost their fear. They became bold. They understood scriptures that confused them before. They got the plan! That's where you are today, waiting to get the plan."

Joanna slowly nodded.

"The Holy Spirit brought power and special gifts when He came to them as both Teacher and Comforter.[6] And you can have the Holy Spirit come to you right now if you want.

"The disciples didn't understand everything Jesus said and you don't have to understand everything right now either. The Holy Spirit brings understanding. You just have to ask Jesus to send you the Holy Spirit. Do you want that?"

She bit her lip and then whispered, "Yes."

"And the Holy Spirit will give you a new prayer

---

5 Acts 1:4
6 Acts 2:1-4

language. A spiritual language. So you can pray easily. It flows through you.

"Just one more thing. Only Jesus Christ can baptize you in the Holy Spirit. If you want to receive the Holy Spirit we can pray together right now, but Jesus Christ is the One Who gives you the baptism."

She nodded again. We began to pray together. I led, and Joanna repeated the prayer.

"Father, I come to You in the Name of Jesus I recognize that You love me and sent Your Son Jesus to remove my sin that separates me from You. Father, I respond to Your love and repent of all my sin. Please forgive me and cleanse me by the Blood of Jesus Christ. By faith, Father, I now receive Your forgiveness and cleansing in Jesus Name. I thank You that Your Word says I am now brought near to You because of the Blood of Jesus Christ through which I enter Blood Covenant relationship with You now.

I renounce the lordship of Satan over my spirit, soul (mind, thoughts, will, intellect, emotions), and my body. I renounce every hold or influence of the devil in all areas of my life, including everything inherited through the generations, because the Bible tells me I have a new Father, my Father God. I am God's child and I only inherit from Him now."

At this point, I explained an influence of the devil included horoscopes, Ouija boards, and psychic readings.

She said, "I've been going to psychic parties and getting readings done."

"I know some people think psychic readings are just fun, but the truth is they are tapping into demonic power. Satan is subtle. He doesn't suggest you get involved in something obviously evil. You would never go for that. He presents evil as good. He is the father of all lies. He deals in deception and trickery. He makes something dangerous appear harmless. Each time you get involved with psychic readings, you get a little deeper into Satan's dark territory. His grip tightens, but you can receive Holy Spirit power that stops the father of lies.

"Jesus Christ tells us everything we need to know when we seek Him. And He tells us the truth. You have an opportunity now to be released from any negative grip of the enemy by rejecting him and rejecting psychic readings. Right now you can ask God to forgive you and He will. And God says when you call on Him, He will answer you."

"Okay. One of my friends warned me not to get into the psychic stuff. She said the same thing you are saying. I won't get involved again." She repented of all occult activity and rejected Satan and all of his lies. We continued to pray.

"Lord Jesus Christ, I ask You to come into my life and I submit totally to You. I ask You to be Lord of my spirit, soul (mind, thoughts, will, intellect, emotions), and my body. By faith, I now declare that sin will no longer

have dominion over me, because Your Spirit lives in me. By faith I am saved, delivered, protected, healed, preserved, doing well, and made whole by the Blood of Jesus Christ.

Lord Jesus, You are the Baptizer in the Holy Spirit. I ask You now to baptize me with the Holy Spirit and fire. I believe by faith, that when the Holy Spirit comes upon me I will receive power and tell people about You everywhere. I believe as I speak the Holy Spirit will give me the ability to speak new tongues. I pray in the Name of Jesus Christ. Amen."

For the first time, Joanna smiled at me. I was cheering inside!

"Okay?"

She nodded.

"Let's pray together with your new gift of tongues. You just let the gift of the Holy Spirit come. You have it now. You won't necessarily understand it, but that is okay. You are just at the beginning of so many new and beautiful blessings now."

I prayed with her with the gift of tongues. Her eyes widened as she prayed a few syllables in her new prayer language.

"That's it!" I encouraged her to keep praying in tongues and pointed out some of her friends at the meeting who knew how to pray through the Holy Spirit and could help her grow in faith.

"How do you feel?" I asked.

"I feel so light," she said drying her tears. She

started chuckling! Then laughing! I noticed that her pupils were no longer dilated! After a long hug she said to me, "I'm going home to unpack my bag."

Joanna is on the road to freedom and equipped to fight the spiritual battle. In my situation, the power God released through Yogi in one moment ended depression. Totally. Is it always like that? Sometimes, people need more prayer and find care for their souls in Christian groups. A woman who struggled with depression and suicidal thoughts for many years told me her story. She overcame, no longer takes medicine for depression, and gives credit to the power of the Holy Spirit. She attends a support group at her church that she finds extremely helpful.

"The Holy Spirit helps me be more truthful with myself. My family background of mental and emotional abuse forged trauma bonds and they became ingrained. Those behaviors bring chronic frustration. It has been painful to look at myself honestly and say, 'I did this.' I have often wanted to give up. Satan traffics in darkness, and when the darkness is in your head the only answer is to willfully bring it into the light. The truth will set you free."

The Holy Spirit has helped her to forgive, and to receive forgiveness. "The Holy Spirit has helped me to mature emotionally, breaking mindsets that kept me from moving forward." As she described the process she has been going through at her faith-based recovery group, I remembered how the Bible describes the Holy Spirit as Counselor. She recognized her need to continue to attend to her inner process as guided by the Holy Spirit. She values the prayers and input of people in her recovery group. And undoubtedly, she adds immeasurable blessings to their lives as well.

Dr. Poland recognized the involvement of church leadership as important to the prevention of suicide. Mental health organizations agree friendship and community are important for people, and church membership offers a sense of belonging. However, Jesus Christ clearly intended the church to offer us much more than a local social club. He modeled for us a body of believers that released His supernatural power whenever the need arose. Christ's followers have been commanded to set the captive free, not just to make them feel comfortable in their captivity.

In the Bridge for Peace community we recognize our responsibility to live the Words of Christ. I often think how God motivated generous friends to share their Florida condo with us. How He was in the midst of arrangements to get us to a pancake house where the simple, straightforward words spoken by His servant with power and authority set this captive free. God fulfills His plan through people. Through us.

I don't know where Yogi is today, but I am forever grateful for whatever price he paid to hear from the Lord as he did. I know he had to spend time in prayer to develop his relationship with

God. I thank God for pointing me out to Yogi. I thank God for sensitizing him, telling Yogi when to speak. Because Yogi waited to talk to us, I had shared my struggle with Ed and he saw the miracle of release, too. I thank God Who told Yogi what to say. I am so grateful Yogi had the boldness to say it, a waiter par excellence. All the good fruit of the Bridge for Peace ministry is added to his account in heaven. In the course of his daily work at the pancake restaurant he performed a life changing service for me. And isn't that exactly what God intends for us?

———◆———

Father God, thank You for delivering us from all evil through the power of the cross of Your Son, Jesus Christ. Thank You, Jesus Christ, for giving to us baptism in Your Holy Spirt. Through You we are released from repetitive lies that plague our minds insisting we "pull the plug." Thank You that Your truth tells us to "plug in" to the power found in You. You freely give us power to be delivered from demonic influence and to deliver others. You give us power to live the dream You put in us, to become more than what we ever hoped to be. You gift us with power to know real peace through Jesus Christ our Bridge for Peace.

TELLING SECRETS

People tell me their secrets. They show me their most exquisite treasure, the secret thoughts of their hearts. Some secrets are hard to talk about, because they are deeply painful or heart-wrenchingly beautiful. Nonetheless, I have found that disclosing a secret, at the right time and to the right person, enriches both lives.

People are like oysters, hiding lustrous pearls in a most tender place, often guarded by an impenetrable exterior. Human hearts store up pearls, our most precious memories. And pearls are amazing in their diversity!

In Tahiti, Ed and I made an appointment to see a pearl merchant. When we arrived at his shop, Raphael asked us questions to get an idea of the type of pearl we were interested in. I was captured by the iridescence and cosmic look of multi-colored pearls, especially the turquoise blues and soft greens reminiscent of planet earth, with tints of purple swirled in like cloud colors after sunset. The non-traditional shapes fascinated me. I had thought of all pearls as round. Not so! I was delighted with the varied exteriors, especially those pearls that appeared to have a small lustrous bump on their round heads!

The pearl merchant provided us with tea, while he privately selected gems to suit our taste. Returning, he invited us into the next room. Pulling out a chair for me at a black velvet-covered table, he graciously motioned for us to sit. Raphael produced a black drawstring pouch and we waited expectantly. He opened the small bag and flicked it. Over a dozen pearls tumbled across the table in a breathtaking kaleidoscopic display!

Whenever someone permits me to glimpse a stunning pearl stored in their heart, the ethereal color and unimaginable shape causes me to catch my breath in awe. Spiritual experience is layered through our stories, as we are spirit, soul, and body. Whether our secret is brimming with grief or joy, we can discover God in the complexity of our stories. God is in the layers, the lustrous depths of our lives. Once we discover His Presence our experience is transformed and we never look upon our story in the same way again.

Jesus advised His followers not to "throw your pearls before pigs; otherwise they will trample them under their feet and turn around and tear you to pieces."[1]

Jesus told His disciples to treasure spiritual understandings as precious pearls.[1] Don't just show them to anyone! The world responds to uncommon personal experiences with disbelief. People insensitive to anything outside of their own understanding may reject and even ridicule those with different experiences.

> **Be wise in sharing memories you have guarded.**

Treasure shared with the right person inspires and blesses. Even that which is not understood can be appreciated. Be wise in sharing memories you have guarded.

As you read this chapter about the disclosing of secrets, consider opening your heart to a trusted person who cares for your soul. Can you find a willingness to expose what lies in darkness to Christ's light? Through the supernatural healing power of God, you can discover unimagined lustrous depths in your experience.

As we explore the realm of spiritual secrets, I thank our Savior, Jesus Christ, for disclosing what He did not have to reveal to us. I thank all of the honest and brave men and women who have shared their journeys and struggles with suicide. And I thank the Holy Spirit for leading us by His counsel

---

1 Matthew 7:6

and shining His light that leads us out of darkness and into freedom.

———◆———

The night of ministry in the harbor town ended on a high note. God's blessings flowed through the worship, the message, and the people who came for healing prayer from the Bridge for Peace team. Many received from the Lord and cried tears of relief and joy. Some people had testified to what God had done, but I hadn't heard all of the stories.

The B4P Team lingered, saying our last good nights in the parking lot. Ed and I drove separate cars home.

The vision God had given us twenty years earlier for a house of healing was underway. I was writing our first B4P Bible course, *Foundation for Healing*. Our itinerary for the year included leading mission teams to Australia, South America, Africa, and Europe, and raising people up in their giftedness in new nations. We leaned on God's counsel for every move. He guided the B4P ministry and our personal lives into a glorious place we could never have imagined.

I settled back for the forty minute drive on the deserted country road. I thought about the B4P team members, the joy of serving together. "Thank you Lord, for what You have done," I said recalling the testimonies of pain relieved and mobility restored.

In my mind I heard a voice, not audible, but a clear impression of a voice other than my own.

Remember Dave and his wife Rachel who was healed?

A picture of the married couple flashed in my mind. I remembered praying for Rachel years before. She had been debilitated by an incurable disease that threatened her life at times, resulting in frightening trips to the hospital emergency room, a terrifying experience for her three young children.

More medication was prescribed, but couldn't control her illness. She also suffered from depression. Her sister brought her to a B4P meeting. She looked small and frightened, with dark shadows beneath her eyes. When she received prayer, she knew she was instantly healed.

She later testified that she no longer took the numerous medications she had needed. Chronic disease and depression left. Her husband Dave said, "Our whole family has a new life. Bridge for Peace has changed everything for us."

Dave had been successful in his career and publicly exclaimed, "I'm giving my money to Bridge for Peace!"

I heard in my head, "He said he'd help, didn't he? You could use some help now, couldn't you?

He is doing well. He knows you and Ed have a lot of demands. Where is he now that you need help?"

"Everything I did, I did for the Lord. God supplies our needs. No one owes me anything." I replied in my head.

"Where are all the people who told you they would be there for you?"

Satan reminded me of the people who had returned evil for good. I remembered occasions when B4P team members had been upset because they felt Ed and I had been dishonored. We had always reassured the team and held no resentment toward anyone.

"My reward comes from God, not men. What I have done has been in obedience to God, not for thanks from people," I argued.

He badgered me, his voice hammered in my head, "What's the point of working so hard? You get nothing out of it! And what about Ed? He's exhausted with the demands!"

"Whatever we have done, we have done for the Lord," I insisted, clenching my teeth, adrenaline pumping through me.

"Why don't you just end it all? Why not just drive off the road? Drive through the guard rail and into the river!"

I pressed my foot against the accelerator for a moment, as if to race away from the voice.

It left. The car felt empty. My mind stilled.

"What was *that*?" I asked myself.

I glanced at the clock. Ten minutes to home. I wanted to get into the house, to be with Ed. Like a dog shaking off water, I rapidly shook my head, as though shaking free of the eerie episode. Attentive to possible threats, I was hyper-vigilant on the vacated road and extra cautious at the traffic lights as I mentally dissected the bizarre experience.

I still felt unsettled the next morning. "God, what was that?" And then I realized what it was. I had met the spirit of suicide.

I was stunned. *Suicide is a spirit?* I recalled the sympathetic overtones, the persistent arguments, and ultimately the aggressive voice of command.

Yes, suicide is a spirit. And it spoke to me!

I was outraged. A spirit, a demon had the nerve to speak to me! And then the evil spirit tried to bully me, suggesting that I "end it all!"

The next week, as a guest speaker at a church service, I sat in the front pew. I was introduced and about to approach the pulpit when I sensed that I was to speak about my encounter with the spirit of suicide.

Following the impression to speak about the spirit of suicide, I immediately heard an objection. "Don't tell people that. What will they think about you?"

I felt a pinprick–the fear of shame. Maybe I shouldn't talk about it. Immediately, I became suspicious.

God trained me to be alert to danger whenever I hear the urgent counsel to "keep it hidden." The suggestion to "keep it hidden" from within me or from another person is a red flag. It warns me to consciously consider the situation before God. The urgent "keep it hidden" always deserves a second look. God's Word says, "Don't be intimidated. Eventually everything is going to be out in the open, and everyone will know how things really are. So don't hesitate to go public now. Don't be bluffed into silence by the threats of bullies. There's nothing they can do to your soul, your core being. Save your fear for God, who holds your entire life—body and soul—in His hands."[2]

Satan wants to engage our emotions. We cannot meet him on that level. I knew the Word told me Jesus Christ had taken all shame.[3] I had nothing to be ashamed of just because I had experienced the voice of Satan trying to tempt me.

The suggestion to "keep it hidden" is a red flag.

Realize that Satan succeeds by replaying the same old strategies. Satan the sly deceiver feigns an interest in preserving our good reputations. Actually, he is appealing to our pride. He passionately reminds us of our importance. Like a publicist, he keeps us aware of appearance.

2 Matthew 10:26-28 MSG
3 Isaiah 53:3-5

"Oh, don't say that," he counsels when we talk about the importance of Christ in our lives. "People will think you are strange. You won't fit in." When we are about to fall into his trap he takes the opposite tack, "There is nothing wrong with doing that! Everybody else is doing it!" He cloaks himself in the attitude of a friend, but he is our sworn enemy until the end. Under the guise of protecting our good names, he will keep us in bondage. When we act on his suggestions, he will turn and accuse us.

I clearly saw that remaining silent about my experience would give Satan an advantage. He exploits all who fear exposure, ushers in shame and self-loathing.

In my case, his plot backfired. His objection made me all the more resolute. I would expose this spirit of suicide in the Name of Jesus and through the power of the Holy Spirit.

That was the first time I spoke of my encounter with the spirit of suicide, but not the last. Listeners related to my story and privately told me their secret experiences with the despicable spirit of suicide.

Then the Holy Spirit astounded me by showing me something new in a familiar scripture. Jesus Christ had been harassed by a spirit of suicide.[4]

For the first time, I saw new meaning in Luke chapter 4. I had heard complex explanations of the passage, but now I found it obvious and absolutely

---

4 Luke 4:9-13

straightforward. The important lesson of hope had been overlooked. The Holy Spirit unveiled the passage to me and God unleashed a spiritual avalanche that rearranged my interior landscape.

In the scripture, Jesus had an extraordinary baptismal experience distinguished by the voice of God. Heard not only by Jesus, but by His cousin and baptizer, John, as well. Jesus is then led by the Holy Spirit into the wilderness where He encounters the devil.

"Then the devil brought Him to Jerusalem and had Him stand on the highest point of the temple, and said to Him, 'If you are the Son of God, throw yourself down from here, for it is written, "He will command his angels concerning you, to protect you, and with their hands they will lift you up, so that you will not strike your foot against a stone.""

"Jesus answered him, 'It is said, "You are not to put the Lord your God to the test."' So when the devil had completed every temptation, he departed from him until a more opportune time."

Jesus did not have one eyewitness to His experience in the wilderness. The spirit of suicide spoke to Him, tried to tempt Him. Jesus didn't have to tell anyone about it. I wonder if the devil suggested to Jesus, "Keep it hidden. Don't tell anyone You heard a voice in Your head telling You to jump! What will people think? If You tell, it will ruin Your reputation. People will think You are crazy. You will lose people's respect. No one will follow You."

I don't know if Satan tried to shame Jesus because of His experience or not, but I do know Jesus disclosed His secret to His inner circle. Jesus had to have told them He met the spirit of suicide or His private experience with Satan would not appear in the Bible.

I think He told His story of spiritual battle in the wilderness again and again, because it is retold in Matthew, Mark, and Luke.[5] In two of the gospels the story is written in great detail as though it was very familiar to them.

Jesus disclosed His secret to His inner circle.

Through Jesus's experience His followers learned how to triumph over demonic spirits. Jesus prepared them through His story.

The Bible doesn't record when or how Jesus told His disciples the story. The following story is biblical fiction, the way I imagine the non-recorded conversation might have happened. Perhaps Jesus had been casting out demons that day and recalled His epic encounter with the devil. Maybe He called a halt to their travel and signaled them to rest along the lakeshore. Perhaps they listened to the water lapping at land's edge as their fire crackled and the sizzling hot sun dropped into the sea.

"Listen," Jesus says, "pray you will not be overcome by temptation, because the Devil stalks his

5 Matthew 4, Mark 1, Luke 4

prey, waiting for an opportune time. After My baptism, I followed the Holy Spirit into the wilderness and the Devil followed me."

"I heard about Your baptism!" Peter interrupts to boast about Jesus to the others. "That was a day! You surprised Your cousin John when You asked him to baptize You!" He looks around the circle of disciples and points heavenward, "The clouds parted and God spoke!"

Peter jumps to his feet. He imitates what he imagines the voice of God sounds like and booms, "'This is My Beloved Son, in Whom I delight!' That's the way to launch a ministry!" Peter claps his big hands together to emphasize his point.

James roars, "Peter, sit down! The Master is speaking!"

Some chuckle, others shake their heads. Peter crouches down and mumbles, "Sorry."

"Tell us, Jesus," the apostles plead.

"I hiked into the wilderness under the control of the Holy Spirit," Jesus stares into the fire remembering the forty days spent alone in the desert. He recalls the words of His adversary Satan who spoke to Him there. He turns His gaze upon His disciples and begins to repeat the details of the conversation no one had witnessed.

"Inexplicably, I stood on the dizzying heights of the temple. The vista was staggering! Beneath My feet was the building most holy to our people, recalling the first tent of meeting in the wilderness. That sanctuary housed the Ten Commandments written on stone by God's finger. In the same chamber lay the Rod of Aaron through which God released miracles and freed our people. And with them was a jar of manna, supernatural food God provided for our people as they trudged through the desert while God taught them they could rely on His promises.[6]

"As I stood on the Jerusalem temple, in that sacred place, Satan spoke. He invades holy ground. He struts past the boundaries of consecrated sanctuaries and imposes his profane presence upon the unsuspecting.

"With his usual insolence he baited his trap with God's own promises. He plotted to trick Me by manipulating divine scripture for his purposes of death. He planned to ensnare Me with God's own promises. Satan, the father of lies,[7] spoke and his voice was smooth, yet commanding. His approach friendly, but like quicksilver became antagonistic. 'If You are the Son of God…' He knows very well Who I am.[8] He slyly called my identity into question saying, 'If you are…' "

The apostles knew Satan would try to confuse them, make them uncertain of their identity to keep them off balance.[9] If he could get that foothold in

---

6 Hebrews 9:2-5

7 John 8:44

8 Luke 4:41

9 Romans 9:7 MSG "It wasn't Abraham's sperm that gave identity here, but God's promise."

their lives, he would drive them to the edge, and strive to push them over, eager to see them fall.[10]

"Know who you are. You are chosen by God. Know you are the children of God, beware the temptation to prove yourself to anyone.[11] Least of all to yourself."

"Satan shouted, 'Jump!'[12] The power of his voice was like a force that would sweep Me off the peak and plunge Me onto the rocks 450 feet below.[13] He hoped to hear My bones crack against the boulders, the sound echoing through the ravine. And then he sneered, '…for it is written…'

"He tried to convince me by quoting scripture, 'He will command His angels concerning you and they will lift you up, so that you will not strike your foot against a stone'.[14]

"He inferred that jumping would show I had faith in God's Word and My unyielding stance against him was cowardice. He insinuated that I did not trust in the promises of God. Beware of Satan's ways. He'll attempt to appeal to you, as He tried to entice Me, by making a bad choice appear good. He'll try to trick you using Holy Scripture,distortingGod's Word to build his case."[15]

---

10 John 10:10

11 John 1:12

12 Luke 4:9 Translated as "Jump" in the *Complete Jewish Bible* and *The Message Bible*

13 1Peter 5:8

14 Psalm 91:12

15 2Corinthians 11:14

Nods of assent went around the circle of His disciples.

Satan intended Christ would die by suicide. He timed his moves[16] to coincide with the onset of Christ's public ministry. Earthly success can be a point of vulnerability.[17] Do not be tricked into presumption.

"Rely on God," Jesus said, "not on what you think you know."[18]

"I answered Satan with the sword of God's Word, an invincible weapon. I quoted, 'You are not to put the Lord your God to the test.' Wield spiritual weapons correctly and cut down lies with truth."[19]

Jesus revealed to the disciples what no man had seen. He wanted them to remember it well. God made sure the episode made it into the Bible —three times.

Jesus could have easily hidden the fact that He had been tempted, but He taught us there is no shame in being tempted. He could have concealed from us that He heard a voice urging self-destruction. Jesus informed them of the devil's command, his demand supported by the misuse of scripture, and his prodding voice urging a death jump.

Jesus knew temptation was a part of life. He also knew that by sharing His victory, he encouraged His disciples to stand firm and triumph over the

16 Luke 4:13
17 Deuteronomy 6:10-18
18 Proverbs 3:5
19 Ephesians 6:17

devil. Sharing His story without shame equipped them to fight.

People often tried to shame Jesus. Those people allowed darkness to use them. Demonic forces strive to engage our emotions. Notice that Jesus based His answers to Satan on scriptural truth, not on His emotions. Jesus's actions show us He did not fear the shame people tried to put on

> ...there is no shame in being tempted.

Him or the judgement. As for those closest to Him, they celebrated His victories over Satan.

———◆———

I spoke about the spirit of suicide at a Bridge for Peace healing prayer service. A man approached me. In a hushed voice he said, "Every day I battle thoughts of suicide. I can't tell anyone. I'm a pastor." Shame, fear, self-criticism, it was all there on his face. Many pastors have shared the same secret with me, expressed the same fear.

Jesus, as Shepherd of His flock, demonstrated that a pastor may hear a suggestion of suicide. Whatever Jesus dealt with, we may need to deal with in the future. Jesus was not afraid or ashamed to reveal His private encounter with a spirit of suicide. Jesus was not rejected by His disciples for revealing truth. I imagine they may have boasted about His victory against the devil.

Christ modeled a community for us where pastors and others can share struggles and be congratulated for courageously engaging the battle. He called us to create a community of confidentiality where people find support and freedom from judgement. A place where people find strength to continue and prayer to overcome.

I applaud the perseverance of those battling with a spirit of suicide. Through their stories we can learn important lessons. Don't give shame power over you. Don't keep the secret, but find a confidant and tell your story. I encourage you to find a safe place to share your private thoughts, your pearls. Care for your soul, mind, and body. Don't overlook the truth that Jesus Christ died to provide supernatural power for your needs. Remember what Jesus Christ modeled. By disclosing that we have heard the voice of temptation to suicide, we truly follow in the steps of Jesus Christ.

> **Find a safe place to share your private thoughts, your pearls.**

Jesus does not indicate that He was at all depressed when He met the spirit of suicide. Jesus had been fasting and mentions His hunger, but doesn't mention discouragement.

When I met the spirit of suicide, I felt stretched by the daily stressors of large projects, but never dejected or depressed. Ed and I faced challenges, but we grew through them and considered them good. I realized from my own experience, that depression is not always a factor in suicidal thoughts.

Depression is not always a factor in suicidal thoughts.

This was confirmed in several interviews with people who heard the suggestion that they take their own lives. During an interview, Karen, a mom whose son died by suicide, confirmed depression is not always a factor in suicidal thoughts.

Bob and Karen talked about their son Rob's suicide. He was a senior in high school. On a class trip, he was found to be carrying a small amount of drugs in his backpack and was arrested. School officials refused to bring him home on the bus. He was released from the police station and set off on his own for home, over 100 miles away.

Karen said, "As he got close (to home), I think it was just too overwhelming for him… People need to know it's not always the depressed. It's not always the person that talks about it... It's the overachiever who fails at something and doesn't know how to handle it."

Bob said, "More times than not, from what I

hear, there is less early warning, less crying out and more bottling up. And I don't think anybody has the answer to that. They say, 'Oh, you should teach boys to be more open...' But our kid couldn't have been more open."[20]

Dr. Poland, suicidologist, says, "When suicide occurs, the most general thing I can say is this simple: It was very likely untreated mental illness or it was undertreated mental illness. We all have to be advocates for treatment being received."

Yes, mental health treatment must be available and we need to practice personal mental health care. Many people in desperate situations find answers through healthcare, but many also continue to flounder.

A woman told me, "I felt drugged out all of the time, even with the many adjustments to my medications. And it never stopped the suicidal thoughts. I hated the feeling the drugs brought on, and that caused me to be more depressed. It felt like a continuous downward spiral. I came to a Bridge for Peace healing conference. I was desperate. I shared with a Bridge for Peace team member who spoke with me about Jesus. I made commitments to Christ and received His promises in my life. I had prayer to get free. Since that day, I am doing very well and am off all medication for eleven months. "

Christianity adds vital tools to the suicide pre-

---

20 Riverhead News Review.Times Review 2017

vention toolbox through the gift of salvation, training on the New Covenant promises, teaching people how to pray, offering an empowerment through the Holy Spirit, education through Bible studies, praying for people to receive supernatural healing and deliverance, and instructing them to operate in the authority of the Name of Jesus to release others from the powers of darkness. This help is not available from sources other than the Body of Christ. Christians know Jesus came to destroy the work of the Evil One.[21]

I wondered later, *Why did I enter into an argument with the demonic spirit. The demonic spirit made a suggestion, I countered it. Why didn't I ignore it?*

I realize when demonic spirits speak, they don't talk to us like we speak to one another. They cast a spell with their voices. In the book of Galatians, Paul says, "…Who has bewitched you?" Satan's voice weaves a powerful spell. He sounds convincing and attempts to stir up unrighteous anger, self-pity, bitterness, pride, and other ungodly emotions.

Demonic spirits lie. They present a half-truth and try to get us to agree with them. They twist words to put us on the defensive.

Don't let the lies of the devil keep you prisoner. When I interviewed Jane, she told me how she found the key to unlock the door to her personal prison.

---

21 1John 3:8

She always knew Jesus Christ and loved Him from a young age. She suffered abuse by her birth family. Her mental state deteriorated when she was thirty years old. She started prescribed medication for her anxiety and depression. She had been in and out of psychiatric institutions, struggling with the spirit of suicide. As she learned more of what the Bible said about Jesus and understood the power of the Blood and the promises she had in God, the suicidal thoughts began to lose their power.

"When I discovered suicide was a spirit, I had a big change. I started to tell the difference between my own voice in my head and the voice of the spirit of suicide. I began to fight it with the power of the Blood of Jesus Christ and win." Jane has greater peace of mind than she has known in many years. She still takes low doses of medication. She now feels "comfortable most all of the time."

Satan wants to keep all suicidal thoughts in the dark. He wants to bring them to mind in his time. He fuels the pain so situations seem larger in recall than they were in actual life. During an interview with Barbara, she told me how thoughts of suicide intruded into her mind during a very routine day. Yes, she had tension in her marriage, but she felt they could work it out. Suddenly she heard the command in her head, "Drive over the cliff!" She had heard the voice before, but it had never been so insistent.

"I said to myself. 'This is not the Spirit of God!'

I didn't know too much about God, but I knew He wouldn't say that to me. I made up my mind. I would never listen to any suggestion of that kind ever again. From the moment I realized that, the voice lessened and then disappeared altogether."

As Karen said about her son, sometimes depression is not a factor. An overachiever can be overwhelmed by shame. Injured pride can become an opening for darkness to enter in.

Jesus Christ modeled transparency in the company of friends. Our safeguard is true humility—knowing who we are, not underestimating or overestimating ourselves. The Word of God reveals that we are unique and precious. We are born into this world with God's plan, the resources from God to support it, and the giftedness from God to fulfill it.

———◆———

Jesus Christ, thank You for doing for me what I could never do for myself. Thank You for staying close to me. Thank You for telling me in Your Word that I have value, for comparing me to a precious gemstone, a unique jewel shining in Your crown. Thank you that I am the pearl of great price to You. You gave everything for me. You help me to share difficult experiences with confidants, give me safe places, and give me strength to bring my thoughts and feelings into Your light. You give me a warrior's heart that will not fail.

Thank you for coming to destroy the plans the Evil One has against me. You guard me from demonic treachery. You train me to war in the spirit and to overcome. You send angels to protect me. Teach me more about the authority I have in You.

In Your name Jesus I command every spirit of suicide to be silent and every dark spirit to leave me. Thank You Jesus for perfect peace. I inherit life through You and You give me supernatural power and an abundant life.

I receive Holy Spirit guidance through You. You fill me with a holy determination to take hold of the life You have given to me as a gift. Holy Spirit, live Your glorious life through me.

I pray in the Name of Jesus. Amen.

SECRETS of the SOUL
and HUMAN SPIRIT

Thousands of years ago, this teenage songwriter lived in poverty and obscurity, yet today her name is recognized worldwide in every level of society. We quote Mary's lyrics and many nations sing her song that begins, "My soul magnifies the Lord and my spirit exults in God my Savior."[1]

At fourteen years of age, without studying philosophy or theology, Mary knew her body held precious treasure. She understood the different roles of her soul and spirit. Her knowing changed her life.

Mary groomed her spirit to hear the Holy Spirit. The source of her holy boldness[2] came from knowledge of hidden realities. Spiritual maturity led her to choose an unconventional path. She agreed to

---

1 Luke 1:46
2 *Holy Chutzpah* by Annette Eckart, Bridge for Peace Publishers

conceive through Holy Spirit power. Unmarried and pregnant, Mary had disobeyed the law. Two thousand years ago, defiance of the rules received swift and harsh punishment. She could expect her choice to destroy her immediate and long term plans and to endanger her life. Despite the risk, she made a potentially perilous choice that inexplicably filled her with an uncontainable joy. She found her purpose in life.

Her life could have been like a footprint on the arid hard-packed earth of her hometown, Nazareth. The prevailing social winds might have erased all traces of her earthly existence. But because of her courageous choice, she will never be forgotten. She changed the world by remaining true to her vision of serving a cause higher than herself.

Mary unlocks spiritual secrets and displays them before us. She exposes the lie that binds humankind to despair. We discover we are more than body, mind, and emotions, and that revelation creates real hope. Recognizing that we have an interior life and making a practice of listening to our inner being, we are guided into an extraordinary adventure. We find the quiet voice that shatters fears. We travel the path of liberation that Mary walked upon to escape the pervasive purposelessness of our world.

We burst bonds of restraint by cultivating a familiarity with the innermost workings of our being. Simply make a habit of deliberately weighing choices with full awareness of our souls' tendencies to dominate and stifle the wisdom voice of our courageous spirits. Mary successfully navigated tremendous obstacles with God's guidance. She found her way by listening. You can, too! Mary reminds us— we have a soul! We have a spirit! We came with a plan!

We have a soul! We have a spirit! We came with a plan!

———◆———

The functions of soul and spirit defined in the first lines of "Mary's Song" draw us to examine the mystery within us.

Our spirit, soul, and body can be compared to a clear glass of ice water. It is extremely challenging for an artist to paint a crystal-clear glass filled with pure water with an ice cube floating in it. Though the glass, water, and ice are three separate components, they are one.

The glass is like our bodies. Remove the glass and the uncontained water spills to the floor, and the ice skids across the counter. The water is like our spirits, the ice like our souls. The water fills the glass. The ice, also water, is distinctive in that it is frozen. But the water and the ice are of the same substance. The glass of ice water is one. If they are separated, they are no longer a glass of ice water. Just so, human beings—spirit, soul, and body—are one.

As Paul tells us in scripture, God Himself has a plan to bring us to complete wholeness in our spirits, souls, and bodies. Our spirits are tasked with the great work of managing our souls and bodies. Without correct order, our lives spill out of control like the uncontained glass of ice water, and we create a mess. If we honor our spirits they will direct our souls and bodies. The result is a peace born of grace with a depth that exceeds human comprehension.

> **Our spirits are tasked with the great work of managing our souls and bodies.**

"My soul magnifies the Lord," Mary said. Her soul views her experience of God through a magnifying lens and enlarges our twenty-first century understanding of who we are. The new perspective offers us hope as to who we may become. Mary's song invites us to look through the lens of our own spiritual vision. We close our physical eyes and see eternal realities. New light emerges from darkness, illuminating our understanding. We too can "see" God; can catch glimmers of our larger purpose, because we are spiritual souls in a body. Yes, we are "spirit, soul, and body"[3] in one marvel-

---

3 1Thessalonians 5:23

ous being! We are whole, not divided, but we can think about our soul as:

- mind
- will
- intellect
- emotions

"My soul magnifies the Lord," Mary said. What does that mean? How does that happen? Why is it important?

Mary used her mind to know God, to recognize Him. By her will she chose to serve Him and to persevere in her choice. She used her intellect to question and learn through mental effort. And with her emotions she loved God. Choosing to align her soul with divine will, Mary allowed the Holy Spirit to shape her into the perfect setting for God's extraordinary work.

Our minds recognize God through one another, nature, life events, dreams, and other means. When we focus our minds on these things to know Him more, we give God a place of primacy in our lives. We magnify Him. If our minds do not magnify God, they magnify problems, make them larger. When we focus on obstacles we find it difficult to recognize God at work in the prob-

If our minds do not magnify God, they magnify problems...

lem. We become short-sighted. We see obstacles as insurmountable, without recognition of God in our midst loving us, guiding us, supporting us, and empowering us to continue to walk forward into wholeness. But some refuse to believe, even when their minds recognize God, as was true of a retired reporter.

I had been recommended as a ghost writer to a successful journalist who was an octogenarian and self-proclaimed atheist. His book was filled with fantastic eyewitness accounts of historic moments and travel, including flights on Air Force One. I asked, "Isn't there one time in your life when you saw God?"

After a brief hesitation, he answered me. "Yes. I saw Him once. During WW II. I was in Africa with a group of reporters. We all knew we had lost the war. It was over. Then Allied tanks came over the hill on the horizon. In that moment, I knew there was a God." He had recognized God, but willfully refused to acknowledge Him.

The will provides power to pursue our decisions, to persevere. God is magnified for us through the political choices of William Wilberforce, member of British parliament and abolitionist whose persistent zeal ended the slave trade. God is clearly seen in the lifestyle choices of Mother Theresa of Calcutta. Stretched almost beyond human limitations, she initiated what has become a worldwide movement that brings dignity to the destitute. Both were opposed by government and society. Exerting the power of their wills, they could not be persuaded to abandon the mistreated and the deserted. Persevering through persecution, they continued to choose God's plan. They married their willpower to God's power and became heroes who restored basic human rights to multitudes.

God created us with purpose. If we withhold our will from God, He cannot work out His glorious purpose in us. But when we give our wills to Him, He will astound us. When our souls say "yes" to God, our wills are functioning in divine order.

God created us with purpose.

Mary used her intellect to ask an intelligent question. "How shall this be…?"[4]

Our intellects comprehend, study, and memorize. Lee Strobel[5] and Michael Rydelnik[6] give us examples of intellects at work.

Lee Strobel, former atheist and investigative journalist, is now an author and pastor. He applied intellectual techniques to disprove the existence of God. He interviewed experts, researched written materials, compiled and compared information. He concluded Jesus Christ was God and submitted his intellectual power to the Holy Spirit.

---

4 Luke 1:34
5 *A Case for Christ*, Lee Strobel
6 *My Search for Messiah*, Michael Rydelnik

Michael Rydelnik, professor and author, did not believe Jesus Christ was God. He used his intellect to read Scripture, to study its meaning, and to debate biblical passages. He concluded Jesus Christ was God and now uses his intellect to help others on their journey.

Many find their intellects resist submission to their spirits. Often our intellects want the final word. The lives of these men demonstrate the supernatural peace attained when we submit our intellects to the knowing in our spirits that commune with God.

Powerful emotions can also seek to dominate us, to derail us from our life's purpose. When the angel Gabriel appeared to Mary, Scripture says she was "troubled" by what he said. Gabriel told her to "fear not."[7] Mary did not allow her emotions to rule her.

Many people live by their feelings. We can be controlled by what we feel like doing, what we feel like eating, what we feel like owning. Emotional wounds from the past can dictate our present responses. My friend Elaine had always been a shy person, but in responding to God she conquered her fears.

Elaine had a practice of listening to God's voice through her human spirit. One day she heard God say, "Feed my sheep." She prepared ten meat and cheese sandwiches and drove to a neighborhood

---

7 Luke 1:29-30

where she had seen people wandering the street dressed in ill-fitting clothes. She saw a man rummaging through a dumpster. She pulled up near him, rolled down the window and asked, "Want a sandwich?"

The man shouted back, "Yeah!" She tossed a sandwich to him and gunned the engine, speeding away. She was nearly shaking with fright, but she submitted her emotions to what she heard in her spirit. Today, the ministry she founded feeds two thousand people every week.

Elaine demonstrated divine order. She did not focus on her emotions, on what made sense to her, or her own preferences. She listened to her spirit and submitted everything else to it. She allowed her spirit to direct her soul.

When the order is reversed, our souls grow desperate for answers and develop insatiable appetites. Constantly dissatisfied, they seek to fill the emptiness. Our souls know we were designed for a purpose-filled life, which we find through the still voice in our spirits. Lacking guidance that directs us to our fulfillment, our souls grasp at any false hope the world offers—money, prestige, and numbing substances that lure us with false promises of happiness. When the soul dominates, life is fractured. It is our human spirits that hear from God and rally the power of agreement in our souls. Starved for our spirits' guidance, we devour junk food from the table of expediency rather than strain forward to the sumptuous banquet set for those who triumph through submission to God. Through the discipline of our souls, we find victory that had seemed unattainable.

Our spirits need recognition. Our spirits bring wisdom to the decision making process. Invite your spirit to speak and then listen!

We know our best life through our spirits. Our spirits hear from God, Who is Spirit. Jesus said, "You will worship Me in spirit and truth."[8] It is our spirits that worship or, as Mary said, "exult" in God.

> **Invite your spirit to bring wisdom to the decision making process.**

Mary shows us how to succeed in what we were born to do. Her words are simple. "Yes, I am a servant of the Lord; let this happen to me according to your word."[9] With these words she gives herself to the Lord—spirit, soul, and body. She yields her mind, will, intellect, and emotions to God's will. These words are the bedrock for an extraordinary life. Adopt these words as a personal motto and discover the power contained in them.

When our spirits glory in God, we experience a deep sense of victory despite real struggles.[10] Negative thought patterns undergo transforma-

8 John 4
9 Luke 1:38
10 *Arrest that Thought* CD by Annette Eckart

tion through the realization of our position in Jesus Christ. We draw on our knowledge of victory through Jesus Christ's resurrection and triumphal entry into heaven where He sat down on His eternal throne. Informed by God's Word, we declare, "We've already won!"

Our inner conviction of supernatural empowerment flows like a bottle of fine vintage wine. Mary and the disciples experienced this in the upper room on Pentecost, when a holy joy exploded through their souls.[11] This becomes our experience, too. Hear the popping of the cork as the Holy Spirit is freed in you through your prayerful "Yes."

We were born for a challenging life that will both terrify and thrill us. Our spirits know that. Failure to acknowledge our spiritual nature fuels an internal division which creates an atmosphere of anxiety, disempowerment, restlessness, and inertia. The internal argument intensifies and we cry out for a resolution. Consumed by an insistent longing for clear direction we cower, plagued by uncertainties and second-guessing.

> We were born for a challenging life that will both terrify and thrill us.

Harmony between our spirits and our souls stabilizes the inner compass, points out our unique

---

11 Acts 2:1-4

direction. A powerful plan of action emerges from a united spirit and soul and we discover we have been swept up in heaven's momentum that propels us down the road we were designed to take. It is as though doors are thrown open to the extraordinary life we were meant to live.

When we first attempt to listen to our spirits, we hear our souls babbling on and on. They chatter about things to do, feelings to resolve, concepts to be explored. They insist, "This is a waste of time!" Most likely we "hear" nothing, certainly not the voice of God! But, at some point, we begin to hear silence.

Silence speaks to us, calms our restlessness. We find ourselves. Direction crystallizes. Choices become easier as we begin to know ourselves. We continue to listen and the silence becomes more profound as our spirits commune with God. We grow to know Him, to understand His love language goes beyond words. Then comes recognition. We know what it is to hear God.

Desperation vanishes with the discovery of sacred space within us. As we continue to honor the divine order of spirit, soul, then body, we notice life falls into place. Confirmations appear. The right people enter our lives. We find courage to let the wrong people exit our lives. Unexpected help turns up. As in Jill's situation.

At 2 a.m. the shrill sound startled Jill from her sleep. Her heart raced, her mind flew to Charity, her daughter away in college. Jill's husband Nick groped to find the phone as it rang again. She heard him rumble, "Hello?"

Jill guessed at the other side of the conversation, praying, her fingers gripping Nick's arm. He turned to her, "It's Charity."

Jill scrambled to dress. Racing out the front door she fumbled with her jacket zipper, subzero wind slapping her face. Nick was already in the Toyota, the interior lights on. Jill saw him bend to the ignition and heard the car start up as she pulled the front door closed to their home, the oasis for their family. Her mind screamed, "What went wrong?"

Parenting was a serious matter for Jill and Nick, family life a priority. They had worked hard to give their children advantages. Charity and her brother both attended exceptional universities in New York City. Charity was independent, intelligent, and had good friends. No one could imagine she would attempt to take her own life. The medical staff had rescued Charity and proposed a treatment plan.

The next morning, Jill reached out to her prayer partners, including Marion. Sensitive to the confidential nature of Jill's need, Marion asked, "May I call Carolyn?" Jill had not seen Carolyn in a year, but knew she was a prayerful woman and appreciated Marion's suggestion.

"Yes, please ask her to pray for us."

Within the hour, Carolyn phoned. She said, "Jill, last night the Lord woke me up. He told me, 'Pray for Jill's family.' I was surprised. I hadn't seen you for a long time, but I got up and prayed for you. It was 2 a.m." The exact time Jill received the phone call from the hospital.

We can imagine Carolyn was tired when the Lord woke her to pray at 2 a.m. She didn't know the need, hadn't seen Jill in a while, possibly she would have liked to roll over and go back to sleep. But Carolyn's spirit was in control of her soul and her body. She responded to the 2 a.m. call she heard from the Lord. We cannot measure the impact her obedience had on the situation, but one day these mysteries will be revealed.

My friend Louise had an experience of the right person turning up and it saved her life. She woke early to the heaviness in her mind and heart that had become too familiar. Worn out by the struggle, she drove to the lake with suicidal intentions. Before she got out of her parked car, she noticed a man strutting around the lake. He lifted a shofar (a twisted ram's horn) to his mouth and blew it—loudly—as he marched. The trumpeting sound split the air and supernaturally shattered the hopelessness that had weighed on her. "I felt freed as he blew that thing! I thought, 'God, You are just too much!' I'm sure He sent that guy down there that morning for me."

Some people find help by dialing a phone number. I interviewed Barbara, who had manned a crisis hotline. She often spoke with people who were suicidal and silently prayed through every call. She said, "I always listened carefully and acknowledged the caller's feelings. Then I asked, 'Can we just put aside your thoughts of suicide for a moment?' Suicide is a permanent solution to a temporary problem." Barbara would get the caller's agreement to introduce a new direction. Barbara would ask if they could imagine a different scenario that could bring resolution. "They would come up with other ideas. Forgiveness, attempts at reconciliation, even making restitution. I just kept praying and waiting and invariably the caller would present their own solution when they stopped considering suicide as an option."

> **"Suicide is a permanent solution to a temporary problem."**

My interview research confirmed Barbara's crisis hotline stories. Those I interviewed that had experienced suicidal thoughts, attempted suicides, psychiatric hospitals, and medicines, told me their lives were either under reconstruction or rebuilt. Katherine, a Christian counselor, told me another heartening story.

Katherine had several clients who heard in their heads, "Just pick up the knife and do it!" She said, "It is absolutely demonic." As she spoke I was reminded of Satan's command to Jesus,[12] "Jump!"

---

12 Luke 4

"One afternoon, I received a suspicious text," Katherine said. "My spirit was disturbed. It just didn't seem right."

Katherine was a woman of prayer and action. She informed the police. The officers arrived at her client's house and rescued her. One moment of delay and they would have been too late to save her life. The woman was admitted to a psychiatric institution.

"My client was furious with me for a long time. But now she lives in another state. She is happily married and has three beautiful children!" Thank God Katherine helped her client to find a different solution.

> In the core of every human being there is a sanctuary, a safe place we can enter.

We have a sanctuary at the core of our being, a safe place we can enter. This interior chapel is not a place to escape from the world, but a space where we make sense of it. Reverence the mystery of life, rather than trying to control it. Cultivate an interior silence. Like Mary of Nazareth, we will discover the next step and find courage to walk in our unique purpose. You alone can write your heart-song, but first you must listen to hear it.

——◆——

Father God, thank You for creating us for eternity. Thank You for our spirits and for our souls. You lead us into wholeness as we align ourselves with Your divine order of spirit, soul, and body. You unveil secrets for us through our spirits and we are filled with hope. Take us beyond our fears to meet You in the silence. You designed us for relationship with You. In that precious bond we come to know ourselves and our purpose. Thank You for giving us new hope. We do not have to live in confusion and fear, but can choose to listen for the counsel of the Holy Spirit. Agreeing with You, we align our mind, will, intellect, and emotions with Your great purpose. We celebrate that You made us to be different from anyone else on the planet. And yet, You formed us to live and work together in harmony. We find solutions to our toughest problems when we submit to Your headship and allow Your voice to speak through us. We put ourselves at Your service and look with great expectancy to the unfolding of Your plan for our future.

Chapter 7

Secret Strength

The tall grass rustled with the hot breeze as Ed and I trekked into the safari park in the shadow of Mt. Kilimanjaro, Tanzania. Our guide, Seeya, led us to a clearing to view a small herd of water buffalo. I heard rushing water ahead. The smell of rich wet earth hung in the air as we wound our way through reeds and arrived at a river. We followed Seeya to the makeshift bridge, a few wooden planks thrown between the riverbanks. He reached for my hand and we crossed. We hiked up the rise. Seeya pointed out safe footholds and cautioned us as we scrambled among the rocks. We entered a hidden canyon where the thundering waters of the powerful falls drowned out every other sound. He pressed on, leading us to a grove that he said was "a favorite spot for giraffes." Gazing up at the gentle creatures, we marveled at how he knew exactly where to find the animals we hoped to see. In unfamiliar territory we need guides, people familiar with the terrain, to take the lead.

We need guides to lead us in our spiritual journey. There are plenty of volunteers for that important position. Voices on the internet, television, and movies vie for attention, hoping to influence us. Some would-be spiritual guides are very dangerous. Persuasive voices call our names to lead us directly into a snake pit. Without spiritual tools in our suicide prevention toolbox, we can be fooled. If we choose an option that falsely guarantees happiness, we find ourselves stuck in a deeper emotional hole. Craving a solution, we grab for anything that promises to numb our pain.

> **We need guides to lead us in our spiritual journey.**

Wise guides can lead us closer every day toward the center of our amazing interior landscape. We can become more aware of our authentic voice, find a clear path, and know inner confidence. Ultimately, we become familiar with our inner guide and are no longer swayed by the intimidation of other bullying voices.

Developing the ability to clearly hear your human spirit and know what God is saying to you requires training, just like any other worthwhile endeavor. We train our souls daily, either intentionally or unintentionally. We constantly hear messages and, until we learn discernment, we believe them according to our inclination. Some of us

> **Stop believing lies by exposing yourself to the truth.**

tend to think we are the best; others of us tend to think we are the worst. We are ripe for lies that affirm our opinion. By either prideful exaggeration of our position or underestimation of ourselves, (or swinging between the two extremes) without truth we are easy targets for victimization. Stop believing lies by exposing yourself to the truth.

Train to build your spiritual muscle. Find spiritual strength for your journey. There are various trails to explore in the spiritual practices marked out in this chapter. The options can help us become more familiar with our inner landscape.

Leave behind every sense of emptiness, uselessness, and the exhaustion of trying. Jesus Christ will meet you right where you are today. We begin by acknowledging our eternal spirits.

I led a seminar in Rome, Italy attended by pastors, seminarian professors, and church administrators. We discussed the importance of the human spirit. In groups of two, the leaders prayed for one another. The instruction was for the one praying to acknowledge the other's spirit and then pray a blessing upon it. Participants all affirmed the importance of the moment, but some felt a real physical or emotional shift, a sense of response in their spirits.

We benefit from the expressed affirmation, appreciation, and blessing of our spirits. Join with a family member or friend. Ask them to place their hand on your shoulder. Open yourself to receive the following prayer.

NAME, I acknowledge your human spirit. God created your spirit to commune with Him and to communicate God's ways to your soul and body. I speak directly to your spirit now. Thank you, spirit, for your unique role in this world. Thank you for directing the soul and body. I bless you as you courageously undertake the function God designed you to perform.

If you do not have anyone in your life right now who can pray with you and bless your spirit, call us at Bridge for Peace and we will be honored to pray with you.

A spiritual director or a Christian counsellor can help you to become more aware of spiritual dynamics and help you to nurture your spirit. Sozo prayer or other healing prayer can be a life-changing event bringing wholeness through supernatural power. Some find their help through

A spiritual director or a Christian counsellor can help you to become more aware of spiritual dynamics.

a spiritual mentoring program available in church. Consider a prayer partner. Having prayed with various prayer partners through the years, I highly recommend this rewarding experience. Commit to regular meetings to pray together and see what God has for you! God has blessings for us, including the preciousness of the cross.

In the old Dracula movies the symbol of the cross is shown to fend off the vampire. That is not a joke. Dark spirits are aware of the power of the cross, they know Jesus Christ destroyed the works of the devil.[1] Christians have been given authority through Christ's triumph over evil at the cross.

The cross is not a good luck charm, it is a sacred sign.

Displaying the cross in our homes helps us to be mindful of God's power and to live our awareness of victory through Jesus Christ. The symbol is not a good luck charm, it is a sacred sign. The sign of the cross is a sign of liberation, as my friend Josephine discovered.

Josephine adopted a boy whose birth parents were alcoholics. He was placed in an orphanage where, tragically, he had been abused. Growing up, the young man suffered from nightmares, occasions of rage, substance abuse, and had brushes with the law. His angry outbursts baffled and frightened him.

---

1 1John 3:8b

He found it difficult to explain his overwhelming feelings. He named it darkness. His mother faithfully prayed for him each night as he slept.

I suggested Josephine anoint his forehead, marking him with the cross. This was not a method to me, but a declaration of faith and of our reliance on God for deliverance. I had learned the importance of this while ministering to a woman who was afflicted by demons and suicidal. She had become unresponsive, as though in a coma. Prompted by the Holy Spirit, I traced the cross on her forehead. All of those present observed a very powerful reaction. The Holy Spirit taught me to treasure this spiritual tool and to be aware of it in my toolbox when God calls me to use it.

Taking my advice, Josephine prayerfully traced the symbol of the cross on her son's forehead each night. Two weeks later she said, "He is totally changed. Keep praying for him, please, but he has not had one nightmare in two weeks. No outbursts. And we have seen other positive behavior changes. My husband is full of hope for our son again. It is truly amazing what God has done."

Beware of witchcraft and superstitious rituals.

Beware of witchcraft and superstitious rituals like knocking on wood to supposedly avert danger. Some jewelry has an occult origin, like the Italian horn and the Greek evil eye. Discard these and objects like them. Get rid of Ouija boards, tarot cards and other occult games. Stay away from horoscopes, psychics, astrological signs, and all other varieties of fortune telling. [2] Horror movies, secret rituals, and talismans are often cursed. If we view ungodly films, participate in secret rituals, or put our faith in an amulet we can be cursed through them.[3]

Rita wore charms she purchased for protection. She suffered increasing anxiety. She sometimes feared getting out of bed. This began the day she put the charms on, however she never made the connection. She removed the talisman, repented, and we broke the curse. The haunting anxiety left immediately. I saw her five years later. She had graduated college and was commencing her master's degree. She was happy and confident, almost unrecognizable from her former state. The effect of the curse was destroyed.

Music can be a source of curses. A man came for ministry, he wanted prayer for his son. As he spoke he began to sob. His whole body shook as he told me his son was addicted to drugs and suicidal. "It all began with his fascination with heavy metal music."

Review the music you are listening to; it is affecting your spirit. Choose music your spirit responds

2 Deuteronomy 18:10 MSG "Don't practice divination, sorcery, fortunetelling, witchery, casting spells, holding séances, or channeling with the dead. People who do these things are an abomination to God."

3 *Foundation for Freedom* Page 68-74

to with joy. Uplifting music with scriptural lyrics can nurture your spirit and activate blessings from God's Word. Many Christian's find music is an effective weapon in spiritual warfare.

> **Review the music you are listening to; it is affecting your spirit.**

We can strengthen our spirits by becoming conscious of God's presence at each meal–three training periods each day. Consciously bless your food. God's given us the power to do it. Thank God for what has been provided. We can become more aware of God's provision in other areas of life when we express gratitude. Pray for what is on your plate and you may find yourself making better food choices.

Apply the same principle to any medications you might take. When you have the prescribed dosage in your hand, pray for it to perform the job it was sent to do without negative side effects. Release the power of a blessing over it. Express gratitude to God for medication that helps restore wholeness.

Christians can also bless the space we occupy at home, work, or while traveling. Command anything evil to leave in the Name of Jesus. Take holy authority over any unclean spirit and tell it to go.

Unclean spirits can enter our minds through what we look at or read. I remember the advice of Walter Wangerin, Jr., an award winning author who spoke to our writers' group. In his teaching, he touched on the Werther Effect. The term refers to a terrible phenomenon observed after the release of a novel in 1774 that described a character's death by suicide. The fiction book triggered a wave of suicides. Professor Wangerin instructed us on the responsibility of writers. He said, "We should ask ourselves, 'Should this book be written?'"

Be mindful of what we look at, watch, or read.

Before buying or downloading material we can ask ourselves, "Should this book be read?" We are influenced by what we read. What is the message? Life or destruction, hope or despair, peace or bloodshed. We literally take it into our souls.

Mental health professionals disagree on the power of the Werther Effect today. However, they do agree on the importance of learning distress tolerance skills. Consider your library shelf at home or in your electronic device. Do the books you find there strengthen your ability to handle stress?

There are books that instruct, biographies that motivate, and inspirational selections of all sorts. There is one book that brings healing to our souls just by reading it. The Bible is filled with words that bring life. It is a source of power that brings wholeness.

Easy reading Bible translations or paraphrases are available today including *The Message* or the *Passion* version. You can view samples online. If you never read the Bible, you might like to start with the book of John. If you do read the Bible, keep reading!

Bible promise books make it easy to find encouraging truths in Scripture and become familiar with God's assurances. Categorized by hope, healing, and other topics, we can find scriptures that speak to our current situation.

To help you explore Scripture, the Bridge for Peace *Foundation for Healing* is a Bible course designed to inform and empower you. Grow in Christ's authority through the lessons in this book and strengthen your spirit. *Foundation for Freedom* is another Bridge for Peace Bible course that can help you understand more about the spiritual realm. Move through it at your own pace at home or join a group. Writing down your own experiences and insights often brings important revelations.

Journaling is a great way to get to know what's happening inside of you. Many people tell me they come to spiritual insights by jotting down their feelings. Journaling our thoughts and our prayers helps many people see more clearly. My friend Penny told me, "I have trouble forming words into spoken prayers, but writing my prayer

> **Journaling our thoughts and our prayers helps many people see more clearly.**

is easy. Also, when I get it down on the paper, situations seem clearer to me. Somehow, I work out my emotions on the page. Sometimes I write a question on the paper and almost immediately I have the answer! I feel like I'm hearing God when I journal." Journaling is a solitary undertaking, but some people like to share their discoveries in a group.

Various Christian groups have been formed around specific interests. They share questions and insights as they follow the structure of the particular materials they are working with. Discussing questions in a group can help us see what we couldn't grasp in private.

Those private moments when we awake to a new day are a crucial time for many. I imagine that is why the Bible often mentions early prayer. [4]

Some people awake to a barrage of negative thoughts. They are frightened before they even get out of bed or they choose to roll over and sleep some more to avoid the voice in their own heads. Keeping a devotional at your bedside can help you.

A devotional is meant to be used on a daily basis. You can find them for 30, 60, 90 days and even a year. Some are in a calendar format. My friend Molly keeps one on her kitchen island and on her dining room table. (She may have them tucked away in other strategic places as well!) You can have a monthly devotional mailed to you in pamphlet

4 Psalm 59:16

or booklet formats. Get one online that will greet you the first time you open your electronic device. There is a great variety of topics, choose whatever interests you. [5]

Encouraging lessons with life applications can appear on your screen daily from various Christian ministries. Short scriptural messages provide practical help. God's Word releases positive power. Wouldn't you like to start your day with an inspirational message?

Fasting is another help that can make us more sensitive to God. We get in touch with our spirits and usually we hear loud complaints from our souls! When we feel the nudge to fast, we can note if our spirits or our souls have dominion over our bodies. Our spirits agree with God's leading, but our rebellious souls object.

Fasting can make us more sensitive to God.

Fasting helps us come into balance. When life feels excessive, the simplicity of fasting can help us find our center. Of course, consult your doctor before a food fast, but there are other kinds of fasting that can be beneficial. We can put aside for a period of time certain types of food, drinks, or electronics. We might realize we need to permanently fast from gossip or negative thinking.

5 *Holy Chutzpah* A devotional encouraging holy boldness by Annette Eckart.

Building meditation into our day helps us grow in the awareness of when we need to fast. When deciding on a meditation practice, be alert to those which are centered in the occult and invite unclean spirits into your life.

Building meditation into our day helps us grow.

Christian meditation practices vary. When choosing a form of meditation consider your personality and lifestyle. Whatever style you choose, begin each meditation period by asking God to bless your time together.

You might choose a Scripture verse or two. Slowly read it out loud three times and then, closing your eyes, deliberately focus on that passage. If other thoughts crowd in, let go of distractions, and bring your mind back to the passage.

You could select a single word and spend some quiet time reflecting on its meaning in your life. Apply the word to God, to yourself, or to the world. Let the word speak to you.

A Bible passage might attract you. Reading the passage, put yourself in the place of one of the characters. Immerse yourself in the scene. What do you discover by entering into the passage? Do you identify or not? Why? Spend time with the passage. Perhaps take up the role of another character. Does this give you a new appreciation of what you read?

If you are a more visual person, meditate for

a time on a picture that you find inspiring. Enjoy looking at it. Nurture your spirit by allowing yourself time to examine it. Notice any response you have to the picture. Take some time to follow that thought or feeling and see where it leads you.

Drawing scripture can deepen your understanding of it.

Drawing scripture can deepen your understanding of it. Colored pencils, pastels, watercolor, or whatever you have on hand is fine for this prayer. Sometimes I use a lap pad; sometimes I sit at a table where I can spread out. Select any appropriate paper and begin to draw the scripture.

Build yourself up by getting to know God and yourself better. Everyone has spiritual needs. Feed your spirit by reserving prayer periods each day, times to talk with God. Enjoying God can take many forms. Just remember, if you are bored with prayer, God could be inviting you to change it up a bit. Get creative with the time you set aside to be specifically aware of God's presence with and in you.

Give yourself the gift of deep silence.

Give yourself the gift of deep silence, a silence that brings a sigh as your body relaxes and sinks into God's rest. God waits to meet with you. May you return to your private spiritual oasis often.

———◆———

God, thank You for wanting to spend time with me. Thank You for deepening my awareness of You every day. You created me with gifts. Please lead me to discover them. I ask You to protect me from false spiritual guides who beckon me to follow dangerous paths. Keep me from false teachers, guard me from false teachings. Be my personal guide Holy Spirit. Send me Your teachers so that I may mature in You and fulfill the purpose for which You created me. I ask for supernatural wisdom to recognize Your signposts at every crossroad. I pray that I may know You more each day. Be my eyes Holy Spirit and lead me on paths of life.

STOP THE LIES

Every lie holds in it seeds of death. Lies destroy life. Lies kill hope. Many people I interviewed for *Spiritual Secrets About Suicide* believed lies. When they accepted the first falsehood, a second one swiftly suggested itself. Deception built a barricade against hope, a fortress of doom. But every lie must surrender to truth. We are saved by the truth. And truth is a person, His Name is Jesus Christ.

Every person I interviewed had felt some relief when they came to know Jesus Christ as their Savior. He sows life into our souls. Nurture that life and you will become strong like a majestic tree. Feed yourself scriptural truth. You will produce beautiful and unimaginable fruit that will deeply satisfy you. But you have to claim what is yours.

Be aware that suicidal spirits want to slip into your mind and live there. Sometimes they show up with a box of chocolates and sweet talk, disarming you with their seduction. Be alert! Ask yourself, "Where does the suggestion lead?" If it is to destruction, slam the door in the Devil's face. Firmly declare to the enemy, "Access denied."

Satan might come like a bully insisting, "Jump!" Jesus Christ exposed Satan's domineering nature and gave us power to reject him. Satan does not control your mind, but he wants you to think he does.[1] You have supernatural power to persevere in the battle. God's power makes you tougher, more persistent than the Devil. Satan is not your boss. Tell him to go and he will run away from you.[2] If the Devil persists, snub him. Jesus is right there with you. Ask Jesus to deal with the Devil when he harasses you.

Many interviewees said that when they came to the realization that suicidal thoughts did not come from their own reason and did not come from God, the intensity of the suggestions dramatically decreased. Some still heard occasional suggestions, but they did not receive them, knowing the source. Expose the liar and stop the lies.

You are not a collection of random parts thrown together. You have been very specifically created in the image of God. You have been designed to fulfill a marvelous purpose in this world. The point of *Spiritual Secrets About Suicide* is to ensure that you have the information to choose truth and to

---

1 *Arrest that Thought*, CD, Annette M. Eckart
2 James 4:7

be supernaturally equipped with God's power. You have become familiar with spiritual tools available to you, now it is up to you to use them. Deliberately and vocally reject the lies that imprison, and embrace the truth that purchased your freedom. Submit your will to God's great purpose for you. Boldly take hold of the power of the Blood of Jesus Christ that was shed for the healing of our wounds, like Felicia did in Brazil.

Our Bridge for Peace healing room was closing for a well-deserved afternoon break in Fortaleza, Brazil. The door had been shut. Felicia burst into the room and shouted, "I have to be delivered! I can't stand it anymore!" She had been suicidal for thirty years. She was ready to receive from God. The team prayed for her in the Name of Jesus Christ and she felt the demonic spirit leave. The next week, her entire family turned up at the Bridge for Peace meeting to thank the team saying, "She is totally changed." Truth sets us free. If the demonic spirit is stubborn, become more determined to receive what God has done for you.

———◆———

Many hear repetitive lies in their own heads planting seeds of death. Satan speaks hypnotically, weaving a spell with his deceptions. The Word of God rips apart lies like a sharp sword, dismantling curses and spells. Receive God's Word like a healing medicine. Let it move into deep places bringing correction to falsehoods. Build a strong life with truth as your cornerstone. Stop the lies.

Applying scriptural truth to your circumstances is key to victory. Discovering your authority in Christ will equip you to triumph in the spiritual battle. Receiving God's promises brings power into your circumstances. Jesus Christ never fails. He is the Word of God. The world will pass away, but God's Word will stand. Fortify yourself for your journey with the Word of God.

The following section identifies common lies people hear. Scriptural truth follows to dismantle the deception and focus our minds. Meditate on the truth. Write it on an index card; keep it in your pocket. Look at it frequently, speak it out loud, and let it become a part of you. The truth does set us free.

LIE: I never should have been born.

TRUTH: "…you shaped me first inside, then out; you formed me in my mother's womb. … Body and soul, I am marvelously made! …You know me inside and out, you know every bone in my body. You know exactly how I was made, bit by bit, how I was sculpted from nothing into something. Like an open book, you watched me grow from conception to birth; all the stages of my life were spread out before you, the days of my life all prepared before I'd even lived one day." Psalm 139: 13-15, MSG

LIE: I can't live with the shame.

TRUTH: "Don't be afraid, for you will not be put to shame! Don't be intimidated, for you will not be humiliated! You will forget about the shame you experienced..." Isaiah 54:4, NET©

LIE: Everyone will eventually leave me.

TRUTH: "'For even if the mountains walk away and the hills fall to pieces, My love won't walk away from you, My covenant of peace won't fall apart." The GOD who has compassion on you says so."' Isaiah 54:10, MSG

LIE: Everyone forgets about me.

TRUTH: "...I could never forget you! Look, I have inscribed your name on my palms..." Isaiah 49:15-16, NET©

LIE: Nobody wants me.

TRUTH: "Even if my father and mother abandoned me, the LORD would take me in." Psalm 27:10

LIE: Things will never change.

TRUTH: "…I am about to do something new. See, I have already begun! …I will make a pathway through the wilderness. I will create rivers in the dry wasteland." Isaiah 43:19 NLT

LIE: I'm emotionally exhausted.

TRUTH: "Come to me, all you who are weary and burdened, and I will give you rest." Matthew 11:28 NET©

LIE: I can't take it anymore.

TRUTH: We are pressed on every side by troubles, but we are not crushed. We are perplexed, but not driven to despair. We are hunted down, but never abandoned by God. We get knocked down, but are not destroyed. 2Corinthians 4:8-9 NLT

LIE: There is no safe place.

TRUTH: The beloved of the LORD will live safely by him; he protects him all the time. Deuteronomy 33:12 NET©

LIE: Tomorrow will be a disaster.

TRUTH: "Seek his will in all you do, and he will show you which path to take." Proverbs 3:6 NLT

LIE: God has too much to do to bother about me.

TRUTH: "And God will exalt you in due time, if you humble yourselves under his mighty hand by casting all your cares on him because he cares for you. 1Peter 5:6-7 NET©

LIE: I don't have what it takes to make it.

TRUTH: "By his divine power, God has given us everything we need for living a godly life... " 2Peter 1:3 NLT

LIE: I will never get out of this mess.

TRUTH: No trial has overtaken you that is not faced by others. And God is faithful: He will not let you be tried beyond what you are able to bear, but with the trial will also provide a way out so that you may be able to endure it. 1Corinthians 10:13 NET©

LIE: I know Christianity works for some people, but it just doesn't work for me.

TRUTH: "But you must continue to

believe this truth and stand firmly in it. Don't drift away from the assurance you received when you heard the Good News." Colossians 1:23 NLT

LIE: I'll never get over this.

TRUTH: "He heals the brokenhearted, and bandages their wounds." Psalm 147:3 NET©

LIE: My prayers don't work.

TRUTH: "The earnest prayer of a righteous person has great power and produces wonderful results." James 5:16 NLT

LIE: I don't need help.

TRUTH: "Two people are better than one… For if they fall, one will help his companion up." Ecclesiastes 4:9–10

LIE: I'll never have any peace.

TRUTH: "Peace I leave with you; my peace I give to you; I do not give it to you as the world does. Do not let your hearts be distressed or lacking in courage." John 14:27 NET©

LIE: Nobody listens to me.

TRUTH: The Lord is close to all who call on him, yes, to all who call on him in truth. He grants the desires of those who fear him; he hears their cries for help and rescues them. Psalm 145:18-19 NLT

LIE: My life is pointless.

TRUTH: "I know what I'm doing. I have it all planned out—plans to take care of you, not abandon you, plans to give you the future you hope for." Jeremiah 29:11 MSG

LIE: God can't forgive me for what I've done.

TRUTH: "But if we confess our sins, he is faithful and righteous, forgiving us our sins and cleansing us from all unrighteousness." 1John 1:9 NET©

LIE: Nobody loves me.

TRUTH: "I've loved you the way my Father has loved me. Make yourselves at home in my love." John 15:9 MSG

The Father loves you as much as He loves Jesus.[3]

---

3 John 17:23

———◆———

John, the football captain whose funeral I had attended, died prematurely and tragically by suicide. His parents still ask why. The mourners cannot make sense of it. No one on earth has the answer. At John's funeral, I heard a whisper in my spirit to share what I knew, to write the *Spiritual Secrets About Suicide*.

When I met the spirit of suicide, it suggested a disturbing lie that I combated with truth. In listening to people's stories, they suffered because they believed, to some extent, a lie planted in their mind. It is time to tell the truth.

Spread the truth that Jesus Christ is a loving, powerful God. Teach others that the Blood of Jesus is for the healing of our wounds. Let's get the word out that suicide is a spirit. There is no shame in being tempted to suicide. Jesus told others about His experience. Refuse to keep the secret. Allow God to use our mouths to bless and deliver captives. The power of deliverance is available through Jesus Christ to be set free. Together we can stop the lies.

———◆———

Holy Spirit, thank You for Your enormous love. You are our Counselor. You will advise us in all matters. You are our Comforter. You console and restore us with supernatural power. You are our Teacher. You will explain Scripture to us and deepen its meaning in our hearts. You are the giver of every good gift. You will awaken abilities that lie dormant in us. You correct our vision of the past and the future. You amplify our hearing so we can listen to God. You empower us to act on what we hear from You. You give us the courage to forgive others and to forgive ourselves. You reveal spiritual secrets to us. You remind us to seek out Jesus Christ, to call to Him, to look for Him in our relationships, in our circumstances. Holy Spirit, you deliver us from lies. Through You we live truth.

TAKING IT DEEPER
STUDY QUESTIONS FOR
SPIRITUAL SECRETS ABOUT SUICIDE

CHAPTER ONE
Why did you choose to read this book now?
"If we lack spiritual knowledge we are vulnerable."
Comment.
This book is about life and death matters. Discuss your understanding of John 10:10

CHAPTER TWO
Who has encouraged or inspired your faith?
Can you share an example of being touched by God's power?
Read Matthew 3:10. Comment on this from a perspective of hope.

CHAPTER THREE
"The Blood of Jesus heals our wounds." Comment.
"The spiritual battle can take place within you as well as around you." Share an example of this.
Physical and emotional trauma can make us vulnerable to lies. Read 1John 4:4-6. Comment.

CHAPTER FOUR
What spiritual tools have you found effective against depression?
Read Acts of the Apostles chapter 2. Comment.
Discuss the Blood Covenant prayer. What struck a chord with you in the prayer?
Pray the Blood Covenant Prayer together.

CHAPTER FIVE
Read Luke 4:9-13. Comment.
How has this chapter encouraged you to battle pressure to "keep the secret"?
The discovery of the spirit of suicide is a proven, crucial tool that preserves life. How would you go about sharing this truth with others?

CHAPTER SIX
Discuss the roles of your spirit and your soul.
Read 1Thessalonians 5:23-24. How does the process of sanctification affect our spirits and our souls?
Read Hebrews 4:12. Why do you think God's Word separates the spirit and the soul?

CHAPTER SEVEN
Read 1John 3:8b. Comment.
Which one of the suggested practices to nurture your spirit might work for you? Why?
Can you suggest any other helps you have used to nurture your spirit?

Pray for each other taking turns to acknowledge
and bless the other person's spirit.

CHAPTER EIGHT

Read James 4:7. Comment on your experience.
What scripture do you find helpful in the battle
against lies? Why?
What have you found most helpful in your group
study of *Spiritual Secrets About Suicide*?

——◆——

Acknowledgements

While climbing higher and higher on a spiral staircase in a church in Jerusalem, I called to Ed, "We are on the stairway to heaven!" In the tradition of Christian mystics, I recalled the interior stair, the silent upward movement of the soul to God.

I brought the image to prayer and was surprised to hear God's invitation to descend. By faith I stepped down into deeper realms where unresolved pain, unhealed wounds, and burdens of grief lived in the darkness. I listened to courageous people tell stories of their struggles with suicide and depression.

The prayers of many faithful intercessors became as candles, bringing Christ's light into the darkness. While I peeled back the bandages uncovering old wounds, the intercessors held a continuous vigil. Thank you to all the prayer warriors from America, to Australia, to Africa, to South America, to Europe. I am grateful to know that God Himself will reward you.

My gratitude to those who shared private experiences with me. You lit up my understanding in ways I never expected. I experienced God's power through your testimony. I applaud your courage. You inspire me. I know you want others to find the cure for their wounds in Jesus Christ. I pray God will use this book to fulfill your hopes.

For Alyssa Montes, Jennifer Searing, Shannon McGarr and Emily Scarbrough, I appreciate your work in suicide prevention and thank you for posing for, shooting, and producing the cover photo for *Spiritual Secrets About Suicide.*

To Dr. Mary Hibberd, thank you for arriving from Texas to teach me how blood heals wounds!

To Fr. Anthony Nabie, you finished teaching philosophy in Sierra Leone and arrived in NY to help. Grazie for your contributions.

Love to my gifted friend Kathy Bolduc for excellent suggestions. You brought both skill and prayer to the process. Thank you for your sensitivity and wisdom that made everything better. We have been up and down the heavenly staircase together many times. I am deeply blessed to be on the journey with you. God bless you for the heavy investment you made in *Spiritual Secrets About Suicide.*

To my beloved Lori Knowling, thank you for sharing your beautiful vision. You encouraged me by declaring that *Spiritual Secrets About Suicide* would be an instrument of deliverance for many people as David's harp delivered Saul from evil. You burned midnight oil to make it happen. You lived Romans 12:1 for the sake of getting this book into the hands of those who need it. And I know you did it for love.

Thanks and more thanks to Kevin McKernan for the text message that inspired the cover and the creation of it, for checking and rechecking. It is a gift to have you at the drafting table, reviewing the details for accuracy. Thanks for walking step by step with me, despite so many other demands. Love you, brother! We share the vision of many names being added to the Lamb's Book of Life through *Spiritual Secrets About Suicide.*

My Eddie, you amaze me by your continual running up and down the staircase! You are always at ease with whatever direction God leads you in. Thank you, dearest, for encouraging me to go higher with joy, accompanying me in every descent, and loving me wherever I am. For the past 45 years we've been ascending and descending together. You epitomize love that never fails. Thank you for praying me through once again. It is true, "We are on the staircase to heaven."

Foundation for Healing
Bible Course

Foundation for Healing Bible Course is the fruit of 20 years of Annette Eckart's ministering healing in the Name of Jesus Christ. Learn and grow as you respond to questions that explore scripture and invite you to reflect on your experience. Read about miracles today in this 12 week course.

Foundation for Healing Companion DVD is conveniently divided into 12 titles that can be shown at weekly study group meetings. Each title has 20 minutes of Annette Eckart's dynamic teaching. This DVD is an invaluable tool to maximize your study experience.

To order *Foundation for Healing*
Bible Course and DVD or other resources
visit our Website www.bridgeforpeace.org
or Call 1.631.730.3982

MORE From Bridge for Peace...

Foundation for Freedom is a challenging study that equips the reader to walk in freedom and release the captive. Annette shares her worldwide experience in deliverance through Jesus Christ. Filled with scripture and personal examples this course offers an opportunity to respond to questions and to process your own experiences. *Foundation for Freedom* provokes thought and action. If you invest the time, apply the lessons, and work the course, it will change your life!

To order *Foundation for Freedom*
Bible Course and DVD or other resources
visit our Website www.bridgeforpeace.org
or Call 1.631.730.3982

CPSIA information can be obtained
at www.ICGtesting.com
Printed in the USA
FFHW010252150319
50968060-56399FF